The Church Meets Judaism

The Church Meets Judaism

by

Otto Piper, Jakob Jocz, and Harold Floreen

Foreword by H. Conrad Hoyer

AUGSBURG PUBLISHING HOUSE

Minneapolis   Minnesota

Sponsored by the

NATIONAL LUTHERAN COUNCIL

Division of American Missions

ABOUT THE WRITERS

Dr. Otto A. Piper is professor of New Testament literature and exegesis at Princeton Theological Seminary. He received his theological training in Europe and taught systematic theology at the Universities of Göttingen (1920-1930) and Münster in Westphalia (1930-33), where he succeeded Karl Barth. Exiled by Hitler, he spent four years in Great Britain as guest of the University of Wales in Swansea and Bangor before becoming visiting professor at Princeton in 1937. He has occupied his present chair since 1941. He is author of a number of books, including *Recent Developments in German Protestantism* and *The Christian Interpretation of Sex*.

Dr. Jakob Jocz, professor of systematic theology at Wycliffe College, Toronto, Canada, was educated in Europe and ordained in the Anglican priesthood in 1935. He served churches in Warsaw, Poland, and London, England, before becoming director in 1956 of the Nathanael Institute, Toronto. He is author of

The Jews in the Bible, The Jewish People and Jesus Christ, and *A Theology of Election.*

Pastor Harold Floreen, a graduate of Augustana Theological Seminary, Rock Island, Ill., is professor at Luther Theological Seminary, Saskatoon, Saskatchewan, Canada. He formerly held pastorates in Chicago and West-New York, N. J., served as executive secretary of the department for the Christian Approach to the Jewish People, Division of American Missions, National Lutheran Council, and taught at Lutheran Bible Institute, Teaneck, N. J. He is author of *The Lutheran Parish and the Jews* and *Pictures of the Way.*

FOREWORD

This book contains the three principal addresses given at the Theological Consultation on "The Church and Judaism" arranged by the Department for the Christian Approach to the Jewish People of the National Lutheran Council, and held at Lake Geneva, Wisconsin, in August 1959.

The Consultation was frankly an experiment in theological orientation. It was arranged to serve Lutheran Churches, but the program was related to the areas of inquiry proposed by the International Missionary Council's studies on the Christian Approach to the Jews. It was hoped that the report of this Consultation could be our American Lutheran contribution to that larger international study.

Personnel included one or more faculty members from twelve Lutheran seminaries in the United States and from one seminary in Canada, related to the National Lutheran Council Bodies, and one professor from Concordia Seminary, related to the Lutheran Church—Missouri Synod. Participants also included the four Area Secretaries serving the Department for the Christian Approach to the Jewish People, three representatives from the departments of evangelism of Lutheran Church Bodies, six parish pastors especially appointed because of their interest in the subject, two church executives with special responsibilities in the general field of intercultural outreach, and four members of the department committee for the Christian Approach to the Jewish People.

The stimulating morning presentations provided ample material for probing questions and lively discussion during afternoon workshop sessions. These questions, a summary of these discussions, and suggestions from the afternoon workshops were reported to the plenary sessions, held each evening.

Full agreement on all points was not reached, nor was this expected. It was quite apparent, however, that new interest in the basic theological questions concerning the Church and Judaism was developed, and new insights into these questions were presented by the Consultation faculty and by other participants. Agreement was reached on five basic principles.

1. In our theology undergirding all mission concern, is the principle that the Gospel is for all men without distinction; and we reaffirm that the love of Christ is the one and only motivation for evangelism.

2. We recognize that the evangelization of the Jews is a matter of Christian conscience and commitment, and that as instruments of the Holy Spirit we must persistently evangelize.

3. It is our conviction that the time is right for a more intensive effort at the evangelization of the Jews.

4. The Christian Church must be made aware of the fact that its spiritual heritage is from the Jews, rooted in God's work within the old covenant, climaxed in Christ Jesus, a Jew, and communicated to us through the early Christian community which was Jewish.

5. We express regret over our neglect of our mission to Israel.

Considerable discussion in the groups centered about the question "Who is a Jew?" It was noted that this is one of the questions before the Supreme Court of the Israeli government which has not been resolved. While none of the groups came to a firm conclusion, it was agreed that whatever the technical definition of a "Jew," the fact of the Jew, and surely the fact of Judaism, is very apparent. Dr. Jocz, in his preliminary address concerning contemporary Judaism, indicated a great spiritual vacuum in Judaism, and called attention to the fact that vast numbers of the Jewish people were not even nominal adherents of any branch of Judaism. He noted also the spiritual groping on the part of many thinking Jews. This

situation presents a new challenge to the Christian
Church. One suggested response to this challenge
was the proposal that the Lutheran World Federation
consider the creation of a commission to prepare and
disseminate an address from the Christian Church
to the Jewish world community.

Discussion also centered around the related question: "What is the present and future historic role of
the Jewish people in sacred and political history?"
Again no agreement was reached, though the suggestion that the Jewish people must play this role
as a separate group, so that there should be a "Gentile" Church and a "Jewish" Church, was not generally accepted.

Other practical suggestions emerged from the discussion groups and are noted here, though it must
be understood that no formal consensus was asked
for or given to these suggestions. We summarize them
in our own words, combining, where possible, two
or more related suggestions into one paragraph.

1. In the Christian witness to Jews, the Christ of
   the Scriptures rather than our systematic theological formulations should be emphasized,
   and the Christ of the Scriptures should be set
   forth in the proper Biblical perspective with
   responsible and full use of the Old Testament
   as well as the New.
2. The "divine mission" of the Jewish people
   should be included as a recognized motivating

factor and as a basis of appeal in addressing the
Jewish people themselves, and in addressing the
Church concerning its responsibility to evan-
gelize the Jewish people.

3. Large segments of the Jewish people are not so
much "for Judaism" as they are "against Christianity," since they identify Christianity with
a negative historical experience of discrimina-
tion and persecution, not only by Christian people, but often in the name of Christ and of the
cross. This provides a definite prejudice barrier
that must be overcome.

4. Contemporary Judaism, of whatever variety, is
much more based on the Talmud than on the
Old Testament, and the Jew, trained in Judaism
of this variety, may have to have this covering
of the rabbinic Talmud stripped from his religious thinking before he can see the relationship between the acts of God in the Old Testament as related to the acts of the same God in
the New Testament.

5. Hebrew Christians should be trained for evangelism among Jewish people since they will
more likely have a congenial understanding of
the Jewish people, their faith and their preju-
dices. They should also be used to train other
Christians in an effective witness to Jewish
people.

6. The study of Judaism and Jewish missions
might well be included as a discipline in theo-

logical education, perhaps within the "missions" requirement.

7. A consultation of the type just held might be encouraged for the future which could include competent Jews among the personnel of the Consultation, provided that the purpose of the Christian Church with respect to its concern for the evangelization of the Jewish people was clearly understood in advance by the competent Jewish scholars who were invited to attend.

8. Additional information concerning the Church's mission to the Jewish people, such as included in Dr. Hoyer's statement "Called to Witness Also to the Jewish People," should be distributed to the pastors of the church through proper agencies.

It was recommended that the addresses and the summary of the finding be published so that it might provide resource material for further study of this topic in the Lutheran Church, and in the wider circle of the World Council of Churches. The published literature could also provide resource material for study in theological seminaries. This book comes as the fulfillment of that recommendation.

H. CONRAD HOYER
Associate Executive Secretary
Division of Home Missions
National Council of the
    Churches of Christ in the U.S.A.

CONTENTS

A PICTURE OF CONTEMPORARY JUDAISM
By Jakob Jocz

THE CHURCH AND CONTEMPORARY JUDAISM
An Exegetical Study of Romans 9, 10 and 11
By Otto Piper

THE GREAT COMMISSION
AND THE PROCLAMATION OF THE GOSPEL
TO THE JEWS

BY HAROLD FLOREEN

A Picture of
Contemporary Judaism

By Jakob Jocz

THE task assigned to me is "a theological presentation of contemporary Judaism." This is a typically
Christian formulation. Jews seldom think in terms of
theology. Theirs is a practical turn of mind—they pre-
fer the concrete to the abstract. There is, however, a
theological aspect in the "picture of contemporary
Judaism"—the aspect of crisis. In this respect there is
little difference between Judaism, Christianity, and
any other aspect of contemporary life. Ours is an
age of crisis. But because the Jewish people is so
much more vulnerable and Jewish life more exposed
to the storms of history, that crisis is more apparent
here than anywhere else.

In order to obtain a picture, one has to take a position and focus the camera at a proper distance. My
own position as a Hebrew Christian, standing between the Jewish people and the Church and be-
longing to both sides, gives me a certain advantage

1

—I look on with sympathy, and yet have the spiritual discernment of a Christian believer.

Our task is to see the actual situation and understand its significance. But no contemporary situation can be understood without reference to the past. This takes us right into the heart of the subject. Contemporary Judaism, as well as Judaism of the past, is always assailed by the basic problem: What is Israel's destiny in history? What does it mean to be a Jew? It is this groping for an answer which underlies the quest of the Jewish community today.

I. HISTORIC JUDAISM

Anyone facing the Jewish community has to face the fact of Judaism. Judaism is not the religion of the Old Testament, but a development from it. Without going into details as to the genesis of the synagogue, here are several basic facts:

1. Seen historically, rabbinic Judaism is an emergency religion. When Yohanan ben Zakkai was smuggled out of the besieged city of Jerusalem in 70 A.D. to found the academy at Yamnia, it was an effort to save Israel's spiritual identity even though his political life came to a tragic end. But this was an emergency measure to tide the people over an interim period. The Jewish people lived by the hope of speedy restoration of Temple worship. To this day

Judaism has remained an interim religion—a religion in suspense. The Hebrew prayer book, the festivals, the ethos of the synagogue, all illustrate this attitude of suspense. The orthodox Jew to this day is in a waiting state: "I believe with perfect faith in the coming of Messiah . . ."

2. From a historic point of view, Judaism was the most potent factor in preserving the identity of Jewry. After 70 A.D., and especially after 135 A.D., the chief task of the synagogue became the preservation of the Jewish people. This was not conceived as a national but a religious task. Every custom, every duty, every precept was utilized for this purpose: procreation of children, special dress, special language, dietary laws, all served the purpose of *apartheid.*

3. Leon Simon, in his book on Zionism, has shown how Judaism did not so much shape Jewish destiny as Jewish destiny shaped Judaism. It means that rabbinic Judaism is the result of the stresses and strains of Jewish life in the Dispersion. The Jewish people without any visible anchorage made the synagogue their home. The emergency measure became the rule and remained such for twenty centuries.

4. The present crisis of Judaism is largely due to the fact that the emergency suddenly came to an end.

II. THE PRESENT CRISIS IN ISRAEL

Jewish hope was centered upon the Return. The
motto of every Jew was: *im eshkoheh Yerushalayim.*
. . . The broken glass at the wedding, the unpainted
spot on the wall, the rising at midnight to mourn, the
fast of tisha b'Av, the frequent prayers for restoration in the liturgy, the longing for the Messiah, all
expressed one thing: the hope of return. The traditional greeting of the Scattered People was: *l'shanah
habah b'Yerushalayim.* . . . The rabbis sharpened the
edge of that hope by declaring that one cannot be a
truly observing Jew outside the Holy Land. The observance of Torah in the fullest sense is possible only
in Eretz Israel.

On a memorable Sabbath in 1948, in the great
synagogue of Tel Aviv, the ram's horn was sounded
to mark the end of the Exile. The Knesset passed the
Law of Return, no Jew need live in *Galut* any more.
He needs no visa, only a ticket and a Jewish nose.
What is the effect upon Judaism now that a religious
hope has been realized?

Paradoxically it created a major crisis within the
Jewish people and within the synagogue.

The creation of the Jewish State put rabbinic Judaism to the test as never before. The synagogue today
faces its greatest trial:

1. The new State is not a Torah-centered, but a
   nation-centered State.

2. Two-thirds of the population is either anti-re-
   ligious or utterly indifferent.
3. Rabbinic Judaism is unable to adjust to the re-
   quirements of modern life.
4. A religious hope which finds fulfillment in history is of necessity a disappointment.

The religious situation in Israel is confused and
fluid, but the nature of the crisis is easily stated:
rabbinic Judaism is regarded by the mass of the population as antiquated and, therefore, redundant. It
has served its purpose, now it is not needed.

We thus face an unusual situation: in the Land of
the Bible, the historic people of the Bible, without a
religious faith, in search of an answer to the question
of destiny: what is the Jewish purpose in history?

This brings us to the Jewish people minus the synagogue. Thousands upon thousands of Jews who do
not practice rabbinic Judaism and only reluctantly
submit to the imposition of rabbinic law in questions
of marriage and divorce, are still essentially religious.
This would apply to Ben-Gurion, himself, who is a
great student of the Hebrew Bible, though for him
it is primarily the expression of Israel's national ego.
At the World Bible Quiz in Jerusalem in August
1958, Ben-Gurion poured scorn upon the rabbis who
"by their tortuous explanations . . . had perverted
the original meaning of the Book of Books." (Cf. the
article by Herbert Weiner, "The Bible of the Israelis,"
in *Commentary*, June 1959, p. 487a.) How far these

two worlds are apart can be seen from the reply of the Chief Rabbi of Tel Aviv to the Prime Minister: Rabbi Unterman affirmed the rabbinic interpretation of Mosaic law with the hundreds of commandments as deduced from the text.

Here is a large, alert, thinking Jewish community left in spiritual vacuum in search of values. This especially tells upon the youth. Dan Jacobson, in an article, "A Crisis of Values, Self-questioning by Israeli Youth" (*Jewish Chronicle*, May 15, 1959), gives some idea of the heart-searching questioning of the brave young men and women who only yesterday were still engrossed in building the State, but who today face the humdrum existence of private life. Jacobson says: "Only now can they ask themselves what it truly is that they have built and fought for. Only now can they ask themselves *how* they are going to live a life which is not supported by the great demands and rewards of a community in continual crisis. . . ."

This is an existential question and because it is existential it is religious; it raises the perennial question of Jewish destiny: What does it mean to be a Jew?

This question became a political issue in Israel in the summer of 1958. It still rages unabated. Hundreds of articles have been written on the subject: *Who is a Jew?* What constitutes a Jew? What does it mean to be a Jew? What is the definition of a Jew?

One of the difficulties arises from the fact that today to be a Jew is not synonymous any more with being a member of the synagogue. How does one define a Jew outside the synagogue? Is the definition racial, cultural, psychological?

Jews are unhappy about a racial definition on historic grounds, on scientific grounds, and in view of the more recent experiences in Europe. Further, a racial definition excludes proselytes who have made Judaism their religion and Israel their home.

Ben-Gurion modified his original definition: "a Jew is a Jew who says he is a Jew," by adding: "and does not belong to any other religion." This, of course, is a logical absurdity, for a Jew is still a Jew if he has no religion or makes fun of religion, but he must not adopt any other religion than Judaism. Such a negative approach has outraged the orthodox camp, for it leaves the way open to racial disintegration by intermarriage.

The answer is not yet; neither is the end of the controversy in view.

III. THE CRISIS IN THE DIASPORA

There is a vital link between Israel and the rest of Jewry. It is becoming increasingly the focal point of Jewish life. The crisis in Israel reflects the state of affairs in the rest of the Jewish world. The origin of the crisis in Israel stems from the Diaspora.

Again we must digress into history to the point when being a Jew meant being a professing Jew. A Jew who fell out of line, as was the case with Uriel

d'Acosta or Baruch Spinoza, was excommunicated. A
Jew who became a Christian was declared dead.
The Jewish community was a closely knit, confirm-
ing, religious community. The break came with the
French revolution at the end of the 18th century.
The gradual opening of the ghetto initiated a movement toward assimilation which is still in progress
at varying degrees. The symbolic figure of re-adaptation is Moses Mendelssohn, who still a faithful member of the synagogue, represents the breaking point
of 18th century Jewry. All his children were baptized
and married Gentiles.

With the opening of the ghetto, Jewry faced the
challenge of emancipated existence. The task was to
adapt to Western society and yet to maintain Jewish
identity. In this process of adaptation there were
many casualties. Some adopted nominal Christianity,
as was the case with Heinrich Heine. Some abandoned religion and became secularized, others tried
to reform Judaism and bring it in line with a more
progressive Western outlook. This is the genesis of
the Reform movement. The result was that it split
the synagogue into many groups.

The cradle of Reform stood in Germany. As early
as 1812, David Friedländer advocated deletion of all
references of a return to Zion in the prayer book and
all vestiges of nationalism. Further reforms were
urged a generation later by Samuel Holdheim and
Abraham Geiger. Geiger went so far as to suggest
the abolition of the age-old tradition of the use of

Hebrew in the liturgy. Political Messianism was abandoned and substituted by the hope of a Messianic era of universal good will. The Conference of American Reform of 1869 and 1885 of Philadelphia and Pittsburgh, respectively, was dominated by German-Jewish immigrants. The Pittsburgh Platform (1885) declared: "We consider ourselves no longer a nation, but a religious community."

Oddly enough this anti-Zionism was shared by Orthodox and Reform alike, though for different reasons. The leader of German orthodoxy, Samson Raphael Hirsch, denounced all practical efforts to bring about the Return. The same applied to the British Chief Rabbi, Hermann Adler, who is reported to have declared in 1909: "Since the destruction of the Temple we no longer constitute a nation; we are a religious communion. We are bound together with our brethren throughout the world primarily by the ties of common faith. But in regard to all other matters we consider ourselves Englishmen." (Israel Finestein, "Emancipationist Apologetics," *Jewish Chronicle*, Feb. 14, 1958).

These statements were dictated by the need of re-adaptation to the new conditions of emancipated existence.

Reformation was founded upon scholarly research, and men like Fraenkel, the Principal of the Breslau Seminary, Samuel Hirsch, Zunz, Krochmal, Einhorn, and Hodlheim were of outstanding scholarship. Their purpose was to define the essence of Judaism in order to uncover its pure, original, classical form. (Cf. Prof. Jakob B. Petuchowski's article in *Judaism*, Spring, 1959, p. 135.) Against the emphasis of orthodoxy upon Mosaic legislation, the Reformers stressed the ethical teaching of the Old Testament prophets. The swing from the practice of orthodoxy to Reform was a gradual process. At the second conference of reform rabbis in Frankfurt in 1845, they still discussed in all seriousness whether a ritual bath taken in artificially collected water instead of "flowing" (living) water was valid. Only by degrees were the old practices abandoned, such as Sabbath observance, dietary laws, ritual bath, etc.

The Reform movement in Judaism coincided with the growth of liberalism in Europe, with the rise of Biblical higher criticism and the discovery of the theory of evolution. It reflects the spirit of the 19th century and reveals much of its weaknesses: facile idealism of progress, exaggerated concepts of man, a philosophical and intellectual approach to God.

The Reformers abandoned faith in Israel's peculiar position in history, faith in a personal Messiah, faith in the uniqueness of Biblical revelation, faith in national restoration of Zion.

To understand the present crisis in the Diaspora we have to bear in mind that recent events have shaken the foundations of both Orthodoxy and Reform alike. Two major events combined to create an upheaval in the mind of Jewry: the Nazi persecution and the establishment of a Jewish national State.

1. The massacre of European Jewry gave the lie to the dearly held tenets of Reform Judaism: faith in man's natural goodness; faith in progress; faith in man's ability at self-salvation.
2. The establishment of the national State raised afresh the perennial problem as to the meaning and purpose of being a Jew.

We have mentioned that both the orthodox and Reform Jews tended to interpret Judaism in purely religious terms. But, while for orthodoxy nationhood was a religious category, Reform gave it a political connotation. Reform Jews, therefore, abandoned the idea of Jewish nationhood and identified themselves unreservedly with the people of their domicile. In Germany they called themselves: Deutsche israelitischer Konfession; in England they were Englishmen of the Jewish faith. C. G. Montefiore once declared that he had more in common with a London cockney who mispronounced his h's than with a Yiddish-speaking Eastern-European Jew. The so-called fifth "plank" of the Pittsburgh Platform (1885) was very emphatic on this point of refuting the national aspect of Judaism.

Since World War II, and most particularly since 1948, a new situation has arisen:

1. The disaster of European Jewry revealed the precariousness of the Jewish position even in liberal and democratic lands. Jews the world over feel that what happened in Germany can

happen anywhere, given the circumstances. They discovered that they have been living in a fool's paradise. There is no security in Western culture. Assimilation does not work.

2. The disaster of European Jewry revealed the superficiality of Western culture. Secularized, pagan, materialistic society is self-destructive. Jews who have blamed Christianity for their suffering in the past have discovered something worse: "scientific" man.

3. The disaster of European Jewry reveals an ethical crisis of first magnitude and calls into question the very foundations upon which Reform is based: the theory of evolution, the natural dignity of man, man's ability at self-salvation.

4. The rise of the National State brought to the forefront the question of historic destiny of the Jewish people—the Reform Jew discovered that he is still tied emotionally, historically, psychologically to the Jewish people.

IV.   THE PRESENT FERMENT

We all live in a time of upheaval. This applies even more so to the situation of world Jewry. Paradoxically, American Jewry with its wealth, its vast organizations, and its well-established political franchise, is spiritually in greater turmoil than any other Jewish community. The state of crisis is reflected in all Jewish publications here and abroad.

A young Jewish writer, Brian Glanville, recently published a novel reflecting Jewish life in a London suburb: *The Bankrupts*. This book aroused a controversy in Anglo-Jewry which is still continuing. The novel expresses the revolt of the younger generation against the crude materialism and the spiritual barrenness of modern Jewish existence.

Brian Glanville, to justify his criticism, published a series of articles in the *Jewish Chronicle*, giving the views of half a dozen young Jewish writers like Peter Schaffer, Alex. Baron, Bernard Kops, Arnold Wesker, and Wolf Mankowitz. All of them take a very critical view of Anglo-Jewry. The controversy culminated in an oral battle at a meeting in which two poets and two playwrights took part. Mr. Silkin declared: "When I call myself a Jew, I do not mean that I am a religious Jew. The Jewish religion is even more rotten and more ossified than Christianity, if that were possible. Anglo-Jewish society was dead, and so was its religion." "Anglo-Jewry in Jeopardy" is a frequent heading in the *Jewish Chronicle*—communal leaders warning the Jewish community against disintegration, conversion to Christianity, intermarriage, religious apathy.

That Orthodoxy in Britain is fighting a losing battle is no secret any more. The Chief Rabbi, Dr. Israel Brodie, who knows the situation better than anyone else, thinks that the decline can be averted by educating more orthodox rabbis: "If every town and townlet in the United Kingdom had at least two men trained at a *yeshivah* we would not see the sorry spectacle of new communities thoughtlessly accepting as a foundation the Reform point of view, which is so definitely negative and which cannot, in any way, ensure a maintenance of Jewish consciousness for any length of time" (*Jewish Chronicle,* April 17, 1959, p. 10). This is the Chief Rabbi's admission that Orthodoxy is in a losing fight.

A similar situation prevails in the United States of America. In addition, American orthodoxy is badly divided. Rabbi Hollander, until recently President of the Rabbinical Council, represents the faction of immigrant rabbis who are uncompromisingly orthodox. But American-born orthodox rabbis, those trained in the Yeshiva University, are more amenable to change in conformity with prevailing trends. A British Jewish writer, William Frenkel, analyzing the American scene, forecasts a serious split in the orthodox ranks in the nearest future (cf. *Jewish Chronicle,* April 17, 1959).

Conservative Judaism, which stands half-way between Orthodoxy and Reform, is the most nondescript movement in American Jewry. William Frankel describes it most aptly in the following words: "Proud of its willingness to cater for all tastes, it has for that reason developed few principles and has little dynamic leadership."

The indefiniteness of the conservative position can be gauged from the "four tested standards" formulated by the Vice-Chancellor of the Jewish Theological Seminary of America in the recent book *Tradition and Change,* The Development of Conservative Judaism, edited by Rabbi Mordecai Waxman, 1958:

1. Scientific knowledge of the whole of Judaism.
2. Judaism as Torah-centered culture or civilization.
3. Klal Yisrael as a challenge to fashion ourselves into a center around whom and through whom Jews of all shades of belief and opinion may experience their common kinship.
4. Innovation without regimentation.

Except for the vague reference to Torah, there is nothing religious or spiritual about these points and there is certainly nothing which could not be acceptable to Reform Judaism.

In a careful critique of the book, the English Jewish professor Leon Roth observes: "Its total effect is to leave the reader with a sense of inadequacy in the movement itself" *(Jewish Chronicle,* "Tradition and Change," May 15, 1959).

Recently Conservative Judaism gave rise to a new trend under the name of *Reconstructionism* under the leadership of Mordecai M. Kaplan.

This new movement emphasizes peoplehood as the focal point of Jewish loyalty and is the American answer to the challenge of national renaissance in Israel.

Prof. Jakob J. Petuchowski, who teaches Rabbinics at the Hebrew Union College, has analyzed the movement in an article in *Commentary:* "The Limits of 'People-centered' Judaism" (cf. *Commentary*, May, 1959, p. 387 ff.). In a few words, his criticism centers round the point that the use of Judaism for preservation of Jewish identity violates the basic principle of religion, that God is to be served for His own sake. A similar criticism is made by Prof. Leon Roth, who sees in Reconstructionism an expression of the spiritual failure of American Jewry. He asks the question: "Has conservative Judaism in America, even in its Reconstructionist shape, anything of its own to offer our generation?" And he adds: "It was born of negation (the negation of Reform). Now in its maturity it seems to see its spiritual life as the adventure of living elsewhere." This is in reference to an admission by Milton Steinberg that "Judaism is the secondary, ancillary civilization of American Jews. . . . Whence it follows that the American Jewish community, for all its size and resources, cannot be expected to maintain itself culturally. To put it bluntly, it is going to have to live on the largesse of other, more intensely Jewish, Jewries." Here is a frank admission, not only of cultural but also of spiritual bankruptcy.

In passing we may add that because of its "survival value," Judaism was always regarded as Jewry's most valued asset. Prof. Petuchowski's appeal to the individual conscience is already a Christian attitude and traditionally derided by Jews.

The resurgence of national consciousness has affected all strata of the Jewish community. Reform Judaism, which was so emphatic in its negation of nationalism, is giving way on the whole front. Prof. Petuchowski remarks: "Reform Judaism and Zionism are no longer, as they were at one time, antithetical concepts and movements. Reform has enlarged the accepted categories of 'religious pageantry' and 'symbolism' to include 'folkways' and Israeli dances." Even the Israeli Day of Independence is being observed by Reform Jews. This new orientation found expression in a recent statement on Judaism as the "historic religious experience of the Jewish people." Note the all-inclusiveness of the statement and the close link with history. Even more explicitly stated is the connection between people and faith in the *Guiding Principles of Reform Judaism* (1957), when Judaism is defined as the "soul of which Israel is the body."

Such is the confused pattern of Jewish life, that the renaissance of national feeling has had little practical effect upon Jewish immigration to Israel. American Jews are sleeping partners in the Zionist adventure. They supply the bulk of the material needs to keep the state alive, but expect others to do the hard work.

Last May (1959) the World B'nai B'rith Convention was held in Jerusalem. Most of the 1300 delegates were from the U.S.A. The retiring President, Mr. Philip Klutznik, in his parting speech, took Mr. Ben-Gurion to task for urging American Jews to immigrate. With great vehemence he declared that American Jews were not in the diaspora but at home.

They "must not be characterized in Israeli minds as available targets for immigration." Mr. Jacob Blaustein, the life-member of the American Committee wholeheartedly concurred: "American Jews vigorously repudiate any suggestion or implication that they are in exile" (cf. *Jewish Chronicle*, May 29, 1959).

Such, then, is the contradictory position of Jewry today: Orthodox who either live in the past, or seek reform: Conservatives who are nondescript; Reform Jews who are falling prey to nationalism; Reconstructionists who are turning Peoplehood into an idol; Americans who celebrate Israel's Independence Day; Zionists who refuse to immigrate.

Monford Harris in an article in *Judaism* entitled "The Bifurcated Life—a Jewish Critique of Christian Thinking (*Judaism*, Spring, 1959), labors to show the bifurcation underlying the Christian faith, and then suggests that the "avid interest of Jews in Christianity" is due to the fact that the American Jew has become a bifurcated person. Without entering upon the question of Christian dualism, we certainly concur with his last point: the modern Jew is a split personality, torn in many directions, without deep convictions and a definite faith in God. This is amply illustrated by such phenomena as Felix Adler's Ethical Cultural Movement, which is frankly atheistic; by Henry Hurwitz's (the editor of the *Menorah Journal*) humanist interpretation of Judaism, which is vaguely deistic; by Liberal Rabbis who doubt the existence of a personal God and regard prayer as mere superstition.

We would sum up our study with a quotation from the already mentioned William Frankel which well summarizes the situation: "There is a searching in all groups for an authentic American pattern of Judaism. The Reform movement claimed in the past that it provided such a pattern, but its current shifts of emphasis indicate that the search still continues. Conservatism is still too vague to be described as a movement with particular philosophy, and Orthodoxy is cleft by the realization by some that a twentieth-century American environment does not permit the flowering of the East European pattern of traditional Judaism."

Here, then, is the "picture of contemporary Judaism." You may wonder about the "theological" content of what you have heard. Let me explain that my purpose was to show the nature of the Crisis. Crisis is a word packed with theological significance. The Greek *krinein* means judgment; it also means decision. Man under judgment is always before decision. A time of decision is a time of opportunity. When man's foundations are shaken he finds himself before the ultimate. This is Israel's opportunity to rediscover God. There are voices in Jewry which point in this direction. Foremost among these is Martin Buber's voice in Israel, and Abraham J. Heschel's voice in this country. I would draw special attention to Heschel's book: *God in Search of Man.* Please note the title, it is genuinely Christian. It is not within the Jewish tradition to speak of God in quest of man. In Judaism it is always man who seeks God. That God is in search of man is the Gospel. Reading Heschel's book one constantly asks the question, "How does he manage to avoid even the mention of Him who stands as the Central Figure in God's quest for man?" Occasionally Heschel comes so near the Gospel that the reader forgets that the author is not a Christian. This is part of the mystery of Israel's hardening.

Here is the challenge to the Church: confronted with a people in crisis what have we to say to the questions which torment the Jewish soul:

1. Who is a Jew?
2. What is Israel's historic destiny?
3. What is Israel's task among the nations?
4. What is Israel's duty: apartheid, isolationism or assimilation?
5. What is the individual Jew's prime responsibility—to himself? to his people? to God?
6. Which is the way back to the source of spiritual life?

In the answers to these questions lies the greatest challenge to the Church.

BIBLIOGRAPHY

Books:

Glanville, Brian, *The Bankrupts.*

Heschel, Abraham J., *God in Quest of Man.*

Jocz, Jakob, *Judaism in the State of Israel.*

Kaplan, Mordecai M., *Guiding Principles* (Reform), 1957.

Kaplan, Mordecai M., *Judaism Without Supernaturalism:* The Only Alternative to Orthodoxy & Secularism, 1958.

Kaplan, Mordecai M., *Tradition and Change*, The Development of Conservative Judaism, 1958.

Simon, Leon, *Studies in Jewish Nationalism*, 1920.

BIBLIOGRAPHY

Articles:

"American Jews Will Not Emigrate," *Jewish Chronicle*, May 29, 1959.

"Anglo-Jewry 'in Jeopardy'—Youth's Lack of Religious Inspiration," *Jewish Chronicle*, April 17, 1959.

Finestein, Israel, "Emancipationist Apologetics," *Jewish Chronicle*, Feb. 14, 1958.

Frankel, William, "No American Pattern of Judaism," *Jewish Chronicle*, April 17, 1959.

Glanville, Brian, "Decay of Anglo-Jewry," *Jewish Chronicle*, April 10, 1959.

Glanville, Brian, "The Man Behind the Pen," *Jewish Chronicle*, December 12, 1958, December 26, 1958, January 2, 1959.

Harris, Monford, "The Bifurcated Life—A Jewish Critique of Christian Thinking," *Judaism*, Spring, 1959.

Jacobson, Dan, "A Crisis in Values, Self-Questioning by Israeli Youth," *Jewish Chronicle*, May 15, 1959.

Loewe, Raphael, "Witch-Hunting" (on the question: Who is a Jew?), *Jewish Chronicle*, June 5, 1959.

Petuchowski, Jacob J., "The Grip of the Past—A Study in the Dynamics of Religion," *Judaism*, Spring, 1959.

Petuchowski, Jacob J., "The Limits of 'People-Centered' Judaism," *Commentary*, May, 1959.

Roth, Prof. Leon, "Tradition and Change," *Jewish Chronicle*, May 15, 1959.

Rothschild, Fritz A., "God & Modern Man: The Approach of Abraham J. Heschel," *Judaism*, Spring, 1959.

Weiner, Herbert, "The Bible of the Israelis," *Commentary*, June, 1959.

Witriol, Joseph, "Who Is a Jew?" *Jewish Chronicle*, May 15, 1959.

Zeitlin, Prof. Solomon, "Who Is a Jew?" *The Jewish Quarterly Review*, April, 1959.

Letters to Editor on the novel "The Bankrupts" are too many to quote, but cf. *Jewish Chronicle* April 4, April 11, May 9, 1958; January 2, 1959.

The Church and Contemporary Judaism --An Exegetical Study of Romans 9, 10, and 11

By Otto Piper

I. THE PROVIDENTIAL ROLE OF ISRAEL

KEEPING in mind the strange ambiguity which characterizes everything the Jews say about themselves, let us turn to what the Word of God has to say about the Jew in his predicament. I have been asked to speak on Romans 9 through 11. It is obvious that exegetes have considered this a very thorny assignment. Evidence thereof is the fact that in some commentaries on Romans these chapters are not treated at all. Other commentaries, who use the time-honored method of interpreting a book verse by verse, are able to find some meat even in chapters 9-11, though in the main we feel they consider this section rather strange. Critics have sometimes advanced the view that actually chapters 9-11 were an alien element in Romans—that Paul had in his desk a little talk on that problem and since he had still some space on his papyrus scroll he decided to add this discussion to his letter to the Christians in Rome.

Now it seems to me that unless these three very important chapters are seen and read in the light of the argument of the whole letter, we miss their meaning completely. But Protestant exegetes have to be reminded of the fact that the earlier chapters have usually been interpreted in terms of Christian individualism; therefore the seemingly unwarranted change from the treatment of individual problems, such as justification and sanctification, to a view of history in which collectivities are central presents great difficulties for the majority of commentators.

I would suggest that, first of all, we view chapters 9-11 in the light of the total argument of Romans before we go into a detailed interpretation of the chapters themselves. Let me also say, right from the outset, that we misunderstand Romans when we consider it merely as a theological treatise.

Paul writes in a very definite historical situation to Christians who were trusted to form the nucleus of the congregation in Rome. Paul doesn't call them a church yet. Obviously they were not organized, but there was enough cohesion among them to meet one another. This means, at the same time, that while this letter is addressed primarily to Christians in Rome, Paul is certain that the Jews in that city would also learn of his letter. That is not surprising because we know that in these early days the Jewish

Christians had contacts with their friends who had not adopted the Gospel. With the close togetherness of the Jewish people, it was obvious that when a letter dealing with such important problems was addressed to certain Jews in Rome, very soon all the Jews would know of it. We see in the letter itself how Paul presupposed that result by sometimes introducing into his discussion the Jew as one who objects to what he has to say, and in general by raising the problem of the fate of Israel as a whole.

What Paul has to say about faith in his letter to Romans is as a rule well known, but one aspect of his view should be mentioned nevertheless, namely that for Paul faith is always man's response to the divine initiative. God does something in the history of mankind and waits for man's response, a response which will be in agreement with the nature of the divine initiative itself. This implies a very important recognition as to the nature of God. The God of the Bible is a God who acts, not as in Greek philosophy merely a god who is. The question of God's existence is not discussed in the Bible and is taken for granted. But the important thing is that God acts, and He is not simply activity or mobility—but a God who acts according to purpose. A great deal of modern theology fails to understand Paul, and I would say the Bible as a whole, by neglecting this element of a divine purpose underlying all that God does.

That purpose—according to the realism that characterizes the Old Testament and the New Testament,

since practically all of its writers are Hebrews—is not
simply God's will to transfer man to some world beyond, but to enable man really to find his place in
the world in which God has placed him and for
which He has created him. That is to say, it is in
the conditions of this world that man is to live according to the purpose of God. This implies, furthermore, that since there is an all-embracing purpose
of God, man lives his life of faith in a historical
sphere. The Israelites were the first to discover that
human life is not simply a succession of unconnected
moments or situations but rather a continuous stream.
Man differs from all other creatures by the fact that
he has a history, and this history is held together by
the divine purpose which gives it continuity. It is
not primarily what man does, nor merely the survival
of the past, that makes for the continuity of history;
but rather, as the Jews rightly point out, their history shows that the continuity is primarily that of
the plan that God has with mankind, and thus with
Israel. Therefore, while there is an element of attri-
tion by which historical accomplishments are whit-
tled away so that even the greatest man is eventually
forgotten, this is not the case where God acts in history. The Bible frequently expresses this fact by
speaking of the faithfulness of God, meaning thereby
not merely that God makes a promise and keeps His
promise, not merely that God's nature never changes,
but above all that God in history constantly pursues
that goal which He has set as He made this world.

It is God who takes the initiative in history, and it is He who assigns man his place in history. God is his Lord, and when God takes the initiative it means that man is not free in his reaction to what God does. Rather his response must be in accordance with the act that God Himself has put forth and with the goal for which man is destined. Paul expressed that fact by mentioning that not only the Jews but also the Gentiles know of the will of God as written in their hearts. Human life is characterized by a *nomos,* i.e., the realization that man must do certain things not of his choosing in order to be a human being. Paul does not deny man's freedom, but that freedom is only a freedom of obedience or disobedience.

A further evidence of the fact that God is Lord of history is found in the moral order of history. The Jews sometimes interpreted that order in a rather naive way. They thought that every good deed would immediately receive its reward, and every evil deed its punishment. The Book of Chronicles, I think, tries in a somewhat mechanical way to apply this scheme to Israel's history. Actually, as we can see, the operation of that order is not so obvious because it is rather complicated. God is not interested primarily in the individual. He is interested in mankind as a whole. For that very reason it is the fate of mankind as a whole in which that moral order manifests itself. That is to say, it is man as a historical being that is accountable for what mankind does. Therefore we cannot speak of history without speaking also at the same time of a final judgment that will confront man. In its light everything that man does is ultimately meaningless. Though that "vanity" may not come out in the act of performance itself, eventually it will come to light. In my opinion one of the blatant weaknesses in modern Protestant theology is the almost complete neglect of the notion of the final judgment of God. We talk so much about the love of God that we forget completely that the New Testament doesn't speak so much of love as of the grace, the mercy, the compassion of God—that is to say, the whole Gospel message is against the background of the divine judgment. Paul has a lot to say about the wrath of God under which the whole of mankind chafes, and he presents the Gospel as man's deliverance from the wrath of God. That is to say, man is not free in what he does, he stands under God's "Law," and he cannot escape God's verdict, because God is his master and Lord.

The most important aspect of the historic outlook of Paul is the universality of history. God is dealing not just with individuals, not with one nation only, nor with the Christian Church only. Rather, Paul points out in Romans 5:12 ff., when he speaks of the contrast between Adam and Christ, that mankind as a whole is the object of God's dealing with this world; it is the destiny of mankind that Paul discusses in Romans. But we would easily misunderstand Paul in his argument if, as is so frequently done in our day, the fate of mankind were interpreted as implying complete disregard of the various groups found in mankind. To Paul it is of the greatest importance that mankind should be divided first of all into Jews and *ethne,* a term which we render "the Gentiles," but the full force of the contrast between *laos* and *ethne* doesn't come out in our terminology. The distinction contrasts a single historical unit, God's chosen people, with the multiplicity of the non-Jewish world, or the nations. That is to say, the only thing the Gentile world has in common is the fact that they are non-Jewish. Yet it is essential that there should be diversity in the Gentile world. We shall see that this feature is of great importance for our understanding of the argument of Romans. As long as you read Romans, as Protestant exegetes so frequently have done, in the light of a humanism that finds in Romans only a discussion of man's faith in general, these specifically historical problems of Israel's existence in history and the role of the Church can not be dealt with adequately in the exegesis.

I said that the Israelites were the first to discover that human life differs from all other organic life by the fact that it takes place in history. Now I would add that another discussion and various reports have brought out one fact—that, on the whole, American theologians are quite willing to take the element of history seriously. But too frequently it has been noticed that, in the Bible, history is invariably seen as differentiated. The strand of history which we might call sacred history (in German *Heilsgeschichte*) and the rest of history, are closely related and serve the same divine purpose but within the diversity that is so characteristic of history. According to the Biblical records, sacred history does not differ from the rest of history by the fact that God is more intimately present in Biblical history than elsewhere. He is present in the whole of human history. Yes, the purpose He pursues in history becomes directly evident in sacred history alone. In other words, the soteriological element in history, and thus in human life, is brought out thereby so clearly that people are in a position to react directly to what God is doing with them. It is God that takes the initiative. Therefore, in sacred history we find a number of events in which God indicates and describes His purpose; e.g., by the way in which God calls Abraham, protects him, befriends him, or by the manner in which He delivers the Israelites from Egypt. This factual basis of the message of the Old Testament and, as we shall see, of the New Testament, is a factor which we must never overlook.

Within that history, furthermore, we find, as Paul will discuss in Romans 9, that God reveals Himself in a direct way. His manifestations create such things as the Covenant, the Law, and the worship of the Israelites. All factors of sacred history, because they are a part of the divine purpose, have lasting significance. That is to say, though sacred history takes place in space and time as does the rest of history, nevertheless it differs from it by the fact that secular

history, as we may call it, is limited in its duration.
Toynbee has reminded us that the highest life ex-
pectancy for a social group is 1500 years, whereas
Israel has already lasted for more than double of
that time. In the same way the Church has the promise that the powers of destruction will not prevail
against the Lord's people. This means that the events
or institutions which have grown up in this process
retain their significance permanently. They retain it,
but they retain it in a specific way. Their reason for
existence is the end which God pursues through
them. In other words, they are not classical works
which have a timeless perfection, and may, therefore, be repeated or copied time and again. No one
would ever think of improving a Beethoven Sonata
or Symphony, for instance; it is perfect as it is. The
same applies to the Parthenon or to the Pyramid of
Cheops, and similar accomplishments. The divine
manifestations in sacred history have, as we have
been reminded, a functional significance. They are
permanent factors in history, but since they are evi-
dences of the presence of the living God, their historical form can and must constantly be changed
without their losing their significance.

Take one example. It is obvious that what the
rabbis consider as the God-given Torah was a legis-
lative code which had developed over a long period
of Israel's history. But this historical origin didn't
preclude the fact that it had its intrinsic unity, and
it therefore remained an authority in its totality.

And furthermore, the student of Jewish history knows that while the rabbis, particularly in the Talmudic branch, insisted on one interpretation of the law, there have nevertheless been quite a number of other types of interpretation of the Torah. This fact manifests the functional character of the Old Testament Law. Take Philo's exegesis of the Old Testament, for instance. While it greatly differs from that of the scribes of his days, Philo was quite sure that he was just as orthodox as the scribes were. Again, Jesus' own interpretation brings out another aspect of the Law.

A further element connected with our view of sacred history is the presence of eschatology in the whole of the Biblical record. Eschatology implies that the meaning of history does not lie in the events as such, but rather in the fact that history is a process that moves toward a goal to be reached, plus the assurance that this goal will be reached because it is God's will that it should come to pass. It is not the intrinsic power of human life or of nature that will bring the result about, as in the systems of Stoicism or Hegel's philosophy of history, but it is the divine purposive will that accomplishes this end. This implies a notion of time that differs greatly from our modern views. We usually interpret time as a line that goes on indefinitely and we say that "now" is the dividing point between what is no longer real and what is not yet real. Actually, according to this philosophy of time, the present time has no existence at all—it is only the transition from the past to the future.

Biblical teaching and Biblical experience present an entirely different view. This is particularly true of the New Testament. When Paul speaks of "now" he does not mean the moment when he is speaking, but to him "now" is the period characterized by the fact that in it the risen Christ carries out His will. This implies in turn that the past is not, as in the mechanical interpretation of time, a dead past that once was and is no longer, but rather that the past, as a part of that divine process of purposive activity, is still at work. This vitality of the past explains the constitutive role which the Old Testament Scriptures play in Paul's argument, and in the New Testament in general. Both for the Jews and for the early Christians, the Old Testament is not simply a document of Israel's early history, or a document of the things that God has done once—as are the chronicles of the pagan world, but rather it is the proclamation of that divine activity which has manifested itself in the past, and which, therefore, determines the whole course of what is to come. For that very reason Paul can interpret the past in a typological way. The mode of God's dealing with man in the past is the same as it is now and ever will be—that is the faithfulness of God. Furthermore, the past discloses the direction in which God is working, though it does not bring to light the goal itself. Therefore, we have the rather strange view of the Old Testament, strange at least

for modern historicism, expressed by Paul in Romans
4 that what is written concerning Abraham is recorded not in order to glorify Abraham, but rather
for our own sake. Through his story we should learn
what the meaning of our own life is. The story of
Sarah and Abraham, in other words, according to
Paul has no significance in itself, but it is important
because it points out the power of God which can
bring the dead to life again, a fact which has manifested itself in the life of Christ. It is God that
raised Christ from the dead, and by the same power
He will also bring about our own life.

From the belief that God has a purpose with mankind Paul derives the idea that holy history is one,
and yet, at the same time the place of diversity. This
is not an idiosyncrasy on the part of Paul—he takes
it from the Old Testament.

The problem that so vexed Greek thinkers, and
which they were never able to answer in a satis-
factory way, was the relation between the one and
the many. If God is one and God is perfectly good,
how is it possible then that there should be a diversified world? The diversification itself seems to imply
imperfection. However, to the Biblical writers the
diversity of this world is an indication of the creative
life in God. Just as the vitality of a person will mani-
fest itself in the fact that he has children, so the vitality of God manifests itself in the fact that He creates
a diversified world. But in spite of the diversity that
characterizes this world, God pursues one end, and

underlying it is the one purpose, redemption. In the answer that Paul gives to the question of the relationship between Jew and Christian, and again between Jewish Christians and Gentile Christians, he does not try to establish a uniform union, but rather shows how, in spite of their diversity, or rather on account of their diversity, they are to realize the same purpose, though in different ways. What is one in God's mind or purpose results in diversity in historical life, yet it is held together by that divine purpose. In the history of the church the Biblical message has been so frequently misunderstood because in a Greek manner people tried to find uniformity. The Roman Church, for instance, insists that the pope is the only one who in an infallible way is able to define the truth of God, therefore there must be a unified and uniform doctrine which everyone must accept. But there are many Protestant denominations, too, that hold a similar view. Since they are certain that they have the true knowledge of the Will of God, all other denominations must be wrong. This kind of mentality is entirely alien to Paul. Yet Paul does not share the relativism of the modern mind, which tries to solve the problem of the relationship between the one and the many by saying that one man or viewpoint is as good as the other; let, therefore, everyone be or think what he pleases. This would be incompatible with the idea that God pursues a goal for man's sake, and that man not only plays a leading role in that process but also has to give account for what he does.

II. THE FATE OF ISRAEL

A. *The Problem*

Let us now turn to the letter itself; we have already spent a great deal of time in discussing the preliminaries.

With the end of the eighth chapter, Paul has reached a peak of vision which seems to remove him so far from practical life that one wonders whether Paul will ever find his way back to earth. It looks as though at the end of Romans 8, with the great theme of God's victorious love, he is already anticipating life in heaven. But it is precisely what he had said in chapters 1-8 that compels him to take up the problem of Israel in chapters 9-11. Paul's reasoning in chapters 5-8 was Hellenistic in character. Paul was speaking there of man in general. But now he reminds himself and his readers of the fact that mankind is hopelessly divided, that the basic division is between Jew and Gentile, and that the church itself is drawn into this conflict.

Paul proclaims the gospel now as it presents itself to the Christian theologian in the light of history. Thus far he has shown that man needs the grace of God—both Jew and Gentile. But is it not his contention that mankind is in a desperate flight, actually a denial of sacred history and all that God has done in the history of mankind? On the other hand, if we really believe that Israel is God's chosen people, if we take the witness of the Old Testament seriously, does not the fact that the overwhelming majority of the Jews not only reject Jesus as their Messiah, but even persecute Jews who become Christians, does not that fact somehow imply that by calling the church into being God has made a new start in history? Do not historical events confirm what so frequently has been said in Christian theology—that Israel has been rejected and its place has now been taken by the church? Paul objects to this kind of reasoning because it would defeat its ends. For it would postulate a God who constantly changed His mind and would do so in an arbitrary way. If God had suddenly shifted from the Jews to the Church, He might change His mind again this year or next, reject the Church, and start in an entirely different way with Shintoism or some entirely new religious movement in the history of mankind. In other words, the current theological view concerning Israel implies a denial of the lasting purpose of God and of His faithfulness.

On the other hand, if you interpret the phenomena in a purely historical way, you are inevitably driven to some kind of relativism. You might say: Men may be fickle, but the Jews loved their own religion and therefore the new movement in Judaism didn't appeal to them, whereas some of the Gentiles adopted it. Ernest Troeltsch took that position. He said, We must interpret Israel's religion as a purely sociological phenomenon, and the Christian religion, too. On a similar basis, Toynbee teaches that man must reckon with the fact that Christianity will become outmoded some day; or, as Tillich says, We have reached the end of the Christian era and now begins a new epoch in history, where a new religion or philosophy takes over the function of the antiquated Christian message.

B. Romans, chapter 9

Over against this humanistic view Paul points out that Israel's history shows clearly that it is not a purely human accomplishment. The fact that God is at work in it comes to light in the prerogatives which in the course of history have characterized Israel. He mentions particularly, next to the Covenant, their spiritual worship, which was so entirely different from anything in the pagan world because there was no statue of God in the temple of Jerusalem. Furthermore, as he points out in chapter 3, they have received the *logia* of God, that is, the revelation of God's redemptive will. The very fact that all these things have happened in Israel's history is an indication of the special attachment God has for them.

But how are we to explain the fact that so many of the Jews nevertheless do not want to become Christians? Paul says the only explanation for it is the working of election, and election is exclusively an act of God. It is not on the basis of what man has accomplished, but rather on the basis of the mercy of God that people are chosen for God's work. Election has often been misunderstood, particularly in Calvinistic theology where this doctrine was interpreted in terms of Stoic philosophy. Thereby God was identified with the *prima causa*. Conversely, to Paul the basic idea of election is the fact that though man was destined for fellowship with God, he refused in his sin to work as God's fellow because he wanted to live a life of his own. That is the way man fell into sin, and thereby he acted contrary to the will and purpose of God.

Whatever, therefore, may be left of moral goodness in mankind, is of relative significance only. Obviously, it would be absurd to say that God is unjust in selecting some and rejecting others, as though some were better than others or as though God wanted to reward the elect for what they had done. Rather, says Paul, what we see in divine election is the fact that God, in spite of man's sinfulness, nevertheless shows compassion with man. He still wants man to reach his appointed end, and that could not be reached if in an indiscriminate way God should treat all men in the same manner. That there is a moral order underlying mankind, God can show only by singling some out for His service in history, while at the same time bypassing others. But a warning must be sounded here. The idea of election has been commonly coupled with the prevailing Protestant individualism which has so dominated the idea of justification. No wonder, then, that election has been understood primarily as individual election. But it is Paul's contention that although God's redemptive purpose concerns mankind as a whole, it affects the historical groups that we find in mankind. Thus, in chapters 9-11, God's saving plan is illustrated by the relations between Jews and Gentiles, and this viewpoint is intimated throughout the whole of Romans. Thus election is closely related to the purpose of sacred history. For sacred history, according to the Biblical message, is not a mere preparation for the future life of resurrection with Christ, but it is primarily concerned with man's life here on earth. Accordingly our earthly existence has a meaning in itself, and that is the consequence of our creation. God had a goal in mind in creating this world, and the theological greatness of Paul manifests itself in his taking that fact seriously. Therefore he interprets the Jewish fate not in terms of individual lives, but as affecting Israel as a whole, and then in turn the Gentiles as a whole.

This interpretation is in keeping with Paul's view of sacred history. Far from being a reward for past performances of man, election is a divine device by which people are called for services to be rendered. Hence originates Paul's problem. Israel as a chosen people had its assigned task here on earth. We can say that in the history of mankind they were appointed to make known and to keep alive ethical monotheism. This idea was for them not a mere theory, but rather a practice. That comes out in the fact that Jewish history implies the will for justice, fairness, and mercy in the dealing of human beings with one another. For Paul, then, the problem of the unbelief of the Jews is one that affects the whole fate of mankind. Israel is not an end in itself—it serves an essential function in God's plan. Therefore God's plan might seem to be defeated at the moment when Israel refused to go with God and respond by faith to what God had done in Jesus Christ.

C. Romans, chapter 10

In the 10th chapter of Romans, Paul immediately raises the question, "If the will of God is interpreted by means of election, does that not imply that God alone is responsible for history and, no matter what man intended, it is obvious God's will has been done?" If that view were correct, it would imply that with the coming into being of the Church Israel as a historical unit had been rejected by God. Paul very categorically says "No," however, and the evidence for his rebuttal he finds in the remnant. The very existence of Jewish Christianity, including himself, indicates the way in which God carries out His purpose. Within the historical units, and particularly within His chosen people, God forms a nucleus which will deliberately assume responsibility for the task assigned to the group as a whole. It is only when you keep this representative role of the remnant in mind that you understand why the prophets never gave up their hope for Israel, though there was so much backsliding and defection within Israel.

Each historical group has specific functions, but

within the group there is a differentiation of offices,
and it is the nucleus that will act representatively
while the other will more or less follow suit. Those,
in turn, who completely leave the group will eventually no longer be able to share the privileges of the
group and the promises given to it.

Concerning the nucleus or remnant, Paul stresses
an implication which we frequently overlook. We
speak often of the nucleus of true believers within the
church, thereby implying that they alone form the
real church. This is typical individualism, in which
the responsibility is ignored which the remnant has
for the whole life of the Church. When Paul calls himself and other Jewish Christians the remnant of Israel,
he interprets its significance in the relationship it has
to the historical task of Israel. They are still within
historical Israel as the group that keeps the Law and
the Covenant and carries out the will of God when
all the other Jews fail to do so. The Jewish Christian,
according to Paul, never ceases to be a Jew. He remains providentially part of Judaism, and he therefore carries on his work primarily for the salvation
(*soteria*) of Israel. The term *soteria* itself has often
been misinterpreted by exegetes. The root *so-* means
integral, full, complete, and is understood in Biblical
language in a functional sense. That is to say, a nation
is saved when in spite of the sinfulness of its members
it is capable of carrying on that function for which
it is destined in mankind. To Paul the whole of mankind is a soteriological texture, in which each group

has its particular function. But he sees at the same time that, on account of their sinfulness, these historical units are not capable of rendering to mankind the service that they should render, and the Apostle would include Israel also under this verdict. On the one hand, he speaks in the present tense of Israel's prerogatives—the fathers, and the revelation, and the worship, and the glory and all these things. While these goods form their possession, yet, on account of their sinfulness, mankind is not impressed thereby in the sense in which they were meant to move mankind. Being destined to be a blessing to the whole of mankind, the Jews by their sinfulness constantly put an obstacle in the way of the realization of that destination. We know how true that is historically. The Jew is a "grand fellow"; however, he also has all the vices of his virtues. He has extraordinary and outstanding qualities, but whether he likes to admit the fact or not, he has also great faults which, while they are the perversions of his special gifts and endowments, are historical realities, nevertheless, by which fellowship with him is rendered difficult. This explains the paradox that ever since the Exile, Judaism has been instrumental in keeping alive in mankind the idea of an ethical monotheism. Yet, at the same time, the way in which the Jews have lived their own religion has contributed greatly to hatred and contempt of the Jews, or, as Paul says, "on account of you the name of God is blasphemed" (Romans 2:24). The saving significance of their religious heritage has not made its full impact on the history of mankind. It has worked itself out primarily in the fields of philosophy and ethics. Because it was on account of the sinfulness of the Jews that their historical mission was frustrated, their salvation, according to Paul consists in the fact that God removes these obstacles which man cannot remove. The grace of God enables a historical group finally to make that contribution to the life of mankind which by its natural endowment it is destined to make.

In this connection Paul will state that the Jewish Christians are the nucleus of Israel. Israel remains a historical entity, held together by the divine purpose of God, which does not change—God is faithful. But it is only through that nucleus that they will be saved, that is to say, be enabled really to be Jews, and thereby to render that service to mankind for which God had destined them. This means, in practical terms, that the existence of a Hebrew Christianity has its providential function in the history of mankind, and primarily in the history of the Jews. We shall see later how the whole problem of the Gentile Christian approach to Israel is clearly seen by Paul.

Nevertheless, Paul continues, while it can be said that God in His election is the one who takes the initiative in the spiritual history of mankind, and so also in Israel's history, this does not mean that man is entirely passive in the whole process. Israel's refusal to accept Jesus as the final manifestation of God's saving purpose is excusable by their ignorance, Paul would say, for the gospel has not yet been preached to the whole of Israel as a historic and ethnic unit. Individual Jews have heard of it, but Israel as a nation has not yet been challenged. This is one of the great problems that confronts the Church. I would say that a great deal of our evangelism among the Jews is one in which the evangelist as a private individual addresses himself to individual Jews, while it should be the Church speaking to the people of God as a whole. This requirement is often ignored, yet to the detriment of the Jew. It has meant that on the whole the Jew has not been challenged as a Jew, and thus has not been enabled by means of the gospel to become a true Jew. The converted Jew, rather than being fitted for the task for which God has destined him as a Jew, has instead been transformed into a Gentile Christian. And therefore, Paul would say, the very fact that so many of the Jews don't want to become Christians, when the development of the church of Gentile Christianity is in the ascendancy, is to a certain extent justified. People sometimes marvel at the tenacity with which the Jews cling to their national existence and to their peculiarities. Paul would say that this is what they should do, because it is what they are made for by God. Allow them as Christians to preserve their peculiar features as we allow it in other nations. In that case, being what they are, and by means of what they are, they should make a saving contribution to the history of mankind.

Nevertheless when everything has been said that might be interpreted as attenuating circumstances for the unbelief of Israel, Paul continues by saying, "Nevertheless there are many individual Jews to whom the gospel has been presented in an intelligent and friendly way and yet they have refused to accept." That presentation of the gospel is in itself evidence that in the spiritual history of mankind God does not treat man in a purely passive way. He does not simply say, "Why, this is your place and you can't do anything about it," but rather He gives him the freedom of decision.

It is for this reason, according to Paul, that Israel must not complain about the fact that in the providence of God their historical function has been terminated, or at least has been interrupted for a while. The very fact that by the will of God the gospel is destined to be brought to the whole of mankind, means that this message of Jesus is of greater importance and urgency than anything that Israel has ever been able to present to mankind. What, nevertheless, always impresses me so greatly here in Romans is that Paul never denies that Israel has a historical mission. Though their national or ethnic existence is not by itself more meaningful than that of any other nation, yet they are indispensable for the spiritual development for mankind. As Paul points out in Romans 11, this function of Israel has not been terminated, though it has been interrupted for some time. Why is that the case? Actually, as Paul says, since God has done all men under sin, one might just as well think that the history of mankind could continue with the Jews playing the leading role. Paul cautions us, however, that if that were the case, the purpose which God had in creating a diversified mankind would be frustrated. The only way we can conceive of a development of the Church and of a Christian history in a world in which the Jews as a whole would have accepted Jesus, would be a mass conversion through which all mankind would have to become Jewish. The differences of the various races would be completely obliterated and the whole world would become a Jewish Christian world.

D. Romans, chapter 11

Obviously Paul is very anxious to point out the providential fact that Israel is one among the privileged nations. It is not the only representative of a true mankind. Their historical significance is not confined to their being truly human, but rather it is dependent on their very particularity. Their Jewishness points to the importance which the characteristic features of all the other nations have for the history of mankind.

According to Paul the cause of sacred history reveals the wisdom of God. The mission of Israel, which is a mission for the whole of mankind, cannot be carried out by means of their making the whole world Jewish. The coming of Jesus Himself and the propa-

gation of the gospel, are acts of God by which He
delivers His own redemptive work from the fetters
by which the narrowmindedness, particularly of the
scribes and the priests, had limited the significance
of His revelation and His gracious operation in Israel.
The only way in which this stagnation in sacred history can be overcome is by God's temporarily excluding Israel from the spiritual history of mankind.
This gives the Gentile world its chance to accept the
gospel in a manner congenial to them and without
Jewishness symbolized by circumcision. Thus the
Gentiles are enabled to fulfill the function formerly
performed by Israel. But since God remains faithful,
this new departure does not mean that in the course
of history one nation gets a chance once and later on
another one, comparable to the way in which modern
historians describe the rise and fall of great empires.
Rather, while Israel must wait for a while until her
time comes again, she has a permanent function in
the history of mankind. The promise given to Abraham will never become void. Thus, for Paul the
church of the future is not a uniform church of an
undifferentiated mankind, but rather the church of
Jews and Gentiles. The specific contributions to be
made by each of the two groups will determine the
nature of the final church. In view of this destination,
we have to take seriously the share that already at
the present moment Israel has in our understanding
of God. In the perspective of universal history, this
means that the Hellenistic interest in a purely intel-

lectual illumination of man, which has thus far characterized the western world and has molded the whole Christian Church, must be supplemented by the ethical realism which is characteristic of the Jewish way of apprehending the will of God.

There are people in our day who say that the Hellenization of the gospel was one of the severest blows that was inflicted on the Church. I cannot share this view. It was providential that, over against the way in which the rabbis had interpreted the Old Testament and impoverished Israel's spiritual substance, mankind should be enriched with the whole wealth of Greek philosophy. The Hellenic spirit enabled the church, in a much broader sense than in rabbinical Judaism, to delve into the wealth of divine manifestation, and to display the insights thus gained in the great systems of theological speculation. But we can also see in our day, and more so than even a few generations ago, that whenever Gentile Christianity is considered as the whole of Christianity we are losing sight of some very important aspects of the work of God. Abstruse as rabbinical exegesis may appear to us, it nevertheless manifests a much profounder understanding of the Old Testament than that of the Christian commentators.

Israel is not a theological idea. Israel is a historical fact, based on the activity of God in their past, and their continuous response to it, and so Israel reminds us constantly of the fact that the gospel, too, has a factual basis. It was inevitable that as the gospel entered into the world of the Gentiles, diversity should become one of the outstanding features of its presentation, because the Gentiles are a heterogeneous group. It was therefore quite natural that the early church should immediately differentiate itself into national bodies—speaking Greek, Syriac, Coptic, Ethiopian, Latin, etc.—as contrasted with the monolithic structure of Israel. But the question then is: What is the principle that unifies these various types of churches, their theology, and their forms of worship?

The reformers tried to answer the question in a way which still is in line with the thinking of the Gentile Christian Church when they said that for the unity of the Church it was not necessary to agree on the forms of worship and polity, as long as pure doctrine and the true administration of the sacraments were maintained. Paul would say, however, that this view still overlooks the very realism of sacred history. The true oneness lies in the common obedient response to what God has done in the history of mankind by sending John the Baptist, His son Jesus Christ, and establishing the Church of Christ here on earth. Looking at the Church in this perspective, Paul sees no need for a uniform theology in the Church. He only demands a common loyalty to the work of God in the Church. But we must not interpret this divine activity in purely static terms, as we sometimes do when we consider the Bible a record of past facts to be accepted as such. Rather, God's

work is the living Word, the whole story from creation to the work of God in Jesus Christ and in the
history of the Church; thus, the constituent facts must
be seen in the light of the goal which God has set
for the Church. That is to say, the churches are united
in their common obligation for the ultimate destination of mankind, and they can accomplish that task
only when they take seriously what God has done
and is still doing through the risen Christ within
their midst.

It is on this basis that we can answer some of the
questions that have been raised in our discussion.
"Who is a Jew?" This question has been asked. It is
quite obvious that Jewishness is not to be interpreted,
as we so frequently do, in merely historical, sociological, cultural, or religious terms. While all of these
elements enter into the description of the Jew, the
Jew is obviously a member of a group which feels its
collective obligation to the will of the God who has
graciously acted in their past, and who has in a
sovereign way fixed their task in this world. This
reflection on their own history implies that in terms
of practical objectives the task of Judaism will be
interpreted in different ways in different places. Some
Jews will say that they are under obligation to
establish and to support the State of Israel. Others
may say, "No," our task is here in the United States.
But these are only the various ways in which they
make their obedience to God's guidance articulate in
the historical world. The task itself and the basis on

which they work, namely the prerogatives which God has given them, do not change. Consequently, since you cannot separate the historical characteristics and the divine mission of the Jewish people, any kind of evangelistic work among the Jews must address itself to the Jew as a Jew. Our task is not to make the Jew a Gentile Christian, but to make the Jew a true Jew. Hence we must first of all enable him to be a good Jew, and only then, also, a Jew who is saved, that is, a Jew who sees what Christ actually means for the historical mission which his people have in the world. One of the most perplexing problems in our work among the Jews lies in the fact that normally in our present situation we cannot proclaim the Gospel to the Jew without saying at the same time, Give up your loyalty to Israel and become a Gentile Christian. Now, as in any national body, there will always be individual Jews who no longer feel that their Jewishness is essential for their own personal life. Thus they will be able, without any special difficulty or pangs of conscience, to forswear allegiance to Judaism and simply become Gentile Christians. But there will be others—and I think that is a majority of the Jews—who will not accept that view and who therefore, unless we approach and address them as Israelites, will be impervious to anything that is said to them in the name of Jesus and the gospel.

Our task toward Israel must probably be divided between the work we do with certain individuals that live on the fringe of Judaism and the work with Israel as a whole. In the light of what Paul has to say in Romans 9-11, it is obvious that the Church has a responsibility not only for the conversion of the individual Jews, but also for enabling Israel as a whole to discover her place in the history of mankind. In other words, our Gentile Christian approach, which is mainly through doctrine, is obviously inappropriate when we approach the believing Jew. In his case, it is primarily our task to make him aware of his dignity, his responsibility, and his obligation as a Jew. It is up to the Church, that is the Gentile Christians, to restore the Jew's sense of dignity. That can be done only by showing him that we recognize him as a branch of God's chosen people, even if he does not become a Christian. This cannot be accomplished, however, without at the same time making clear to the Jew that it is not from his attainments in the field of learning or economic life, or his political achievements in Israel that he has derived his true dignity. Since success in these realms will come and go with the flux of time, he should never rest his sense of dignity on them. He must rely on the fact that God has chosen him for a task to be performed for the whole of mankind. With such an approach I think we have a common basis on which we can talk with the Jew. The fact, furthermore, that in our day a number of congregations of Hebrew Christians are in existence is of the greatest practical significance. Just as Paul thought that the Jewish Christians in his day were the providential nucleus of the whole Jewish people who would keep alive the understanding of Israel's mission and task, so I think it is in our day.

Mission work among the Jews is such a difficult and frustrating activity, because with our Gentile background most of us simply don't see what actually is central in Jewish existence. That is why I think that not only the work of Jewish Christians in individual evangelism is important, but also the existence of Jewish Christian congregations. These groups, which are Jewish in character and who keep the law, be it in the orthodox, the conservative, or the reformed way, demonstrate by their very existence that they are proud of being rooted in Israel, and are willing to assume the task which was assigned to the whole people. We should also keep in mind that all our evangelistic work among the Jews has only temporary significance because, in the providence of God, Israel as a whole will eventually be won over. But according to Paul there can be no doubt that Christianity has a responsibility for Israel, and I would go considerably farther than those who say that such responsibility is discharged by distributing New Testaments among the Jews. Having been granted the full vision of God's purpose with mankind, the Church is in a position to tell the Jew what he is meant to be and to remind him of the fact that he has a divine mission in this world. When people say that Judaism is only a passing phenomenon in the history of human religions, and that it will disappear some day, their view is not supported by

Paul. According to Paul there will eventually be a united church for the entire mankind, but it will be a differentiated one, because the realism of the Jew and all the characteristics of the other nations will play their role in its history. Thus alone will the united Church of the future be the Church of the whole of mankind.

Paul has no reason to discuss in detail what characterizes the various members of the Gentile world. From his statements we can conclude this, however. Historically speaking, Israel is but one nation among the multiplicity of nations, but on account of the place which it occupies in sacred history, the significance of her individual character greatly excels that of the Gentiles. Though sharing the limitations of a particular nation, Israel, as a branch of the chosen people, enters into the history of mankind as one whose specific characteristics are deemed necessary by God for the purpose He wants to realize in the history of mankind. Things are different in the role of the Gentiles. Each nation has its own particular features and thus, when converted to Christianity, makes its respective contribution to the history of Christianity. Yet we cannot say that for that reason American Christianity or German Christianity is more important for the progress of the Church than, for instance, Assyrian Christianity or Coptic Christianity, branches of the Church which for all practical purposes have now lost their significance in sacred history and, therefore, in the history of the Church. In turn, their historical significance is dependent on their allegiance to the Bible and its God. In other words, to be effective, all the Gentile churches must return to the realism of the Hebrew religion. On account of this foundational role of Israel, we cannot say that the relationship between the Church and Israel is truly described by an ellipse with two foci, as modern Jewish writers like to advocate. Such an image would imply that the two are equally necessary, yet should be kept apart. By God's will they are actually meant to work on each other. It has been pointed out how much the emancipation of the Jews in western Europe has meant for the whole development of Judaism. By coming into contact with the civilization and culture that the Gentile church had created in the western world, the Jews were enormously enriched in their whole life. As Dr. Jocz points out, the very crisis in which the Jews find themselves theologically at the present time is the result of the intimate contact that they have had with the whole world of Gentile Christianity. It is not left to the discretion of the Christian or the Jew to decide in which way he will react to this historical situation. This encounter is a phase of sacred history which demands of both of them that they accept their common responsibility by supplementing each other, while working for their common goal.

The question has been raised whether the approach to the Jews should be theocentric or Christocentric. Actually it seems to me that this is too narrow a way of stating the problem. What Israel needs is not a new theology, but rather the clear and frank realization of her intrinsic spiritual weakness, which can be overcome only by the grace of God, the grace of God as shown in the work of Jesus Christ. It is the way in which Israel proudly conceives of herself as a self-contained entity that makes her unable to work for the goal for which she is called, whereas it is the very humility, that we learn from Jesus Christ which will enable us to accept our true dignity as consisting in being God's instruments for the salvation of mankind.

The Great Commission
and the Proclamation of
the Gospel to the Jews

By Harold Floreen

THE two previous chapters dealt primarily with the Jews. The subject of this presentation, on the other hand, is the Church in its responsibility to Jewish people. It would be difficult, however, to discuss this matter intelligently without some reference to the background of the present consultation.

We must go back to the First Assembly of the World Council of Churches at Amsterdam, Holland, in 1948. This Assembly received a well-developed report on the relation of the Church to the Jews, commended it to the member churches for their consideration, and also passed on to them a number of recommendations. In addition, a mandate was given to the Central Committee of the World Council of Churches to give further study to the "many complex problems which exist in the field of relations between Christians and Jews," certain topics being particularly pinpointed for such study.

The first of the recommendations referred to the member churches is particularly relevant to our present concern, for it urged those churches to "seek to recover the universality of our Lord's commission by including the Jewish people in their evangelistic work."

The mandate to the Central Committee for further study was implemented through a study conference arranged under the joint auspices of the American Section of the Committee of the Christian Approach to the Jews of the International Missionary Council and the Committee on the Christian Approach to the Jews under the Division of Home Missions of the National Council of Churches. The conference was held in August, 1954, shortly before the Evanston Assembly, Lake Geneva, Wisconsin.

The findings and recommendations of the study conference were sent on to the Evanston Assembly, where they struck fire. The report was not accepted, but was referred to the Central Committee for further study. The day was saved in part by an opinion presented by a minority group of which Dr. Joseph Sittler was the spokesman.

In the implementation of the Evanston Assembly's mandate for further study, it fell to the lot of the Joint Committee of the World Council of Churches and the International Missionary Council to arrange for a study conference prior to the next Assembly. An international theological consultation was arranged at Bossey, Switzerland, in the Fall of 1956.

Great difficulty was experienced in securing American representation. In the final analysis, Dr. H. Conrad Hoyer was the only American representative who attended.

In consideration of the very great responsibility of the American churches in this field, it was deemed necessary to arrange for an American theological consultation which would reflect the various facets of opinions in American church circles. When preliminary discussions were held as to the nature of such a consultation, American representatives of the World Council of Churches and the International Missionary Council seriously questioned whether calling one top-level meeting involving outstanding theologians and resource people would be the answer. Because we Americans have not generally done a great deal of basic thinking concerning our responsibility to the Jews, especially from the Biblical and theological viewpoints, it was doubted that a genuine and mature consensus could be achieved in so short a time. Moreover, opinions vary, not only between denominations, but sectionally as well. For example, one might expect a quite different attitude in New England from that held in the South or in the Mid-west.

In consideration of these factors, it was deemed advisable to set up a study program which would encourage consultations at theological centers in various parts of the nation. The actual implementation of the study program was placed under the Department of Evangelism of the National Council of Churches in a special committee headed by Rev. Lawrence W. Halvorson. Rev. Göte Hedenquist, Executive Secretary of the International Missionary Council's Committee on the Christian Approach to the Jews, came over especially from Sweden to assist in encouraging the holding of theological study conferences.

The special committee under the Department of Evangelism decided that, in addition to consultations at leading theological centers, study conferences representing individual denominations would be highly desirable. The present consultation in which we are now engaged is a response to this opinion. It is important, however, that we as Lutherans should study our relation to the Jews in order to clarify our own position. Should our opinions or findings prove helpful to the church at large, we shall be doubly grateful.

I. THE LORDSHIP AND AUTHORITY OF CHRIST

A. Direct Challenges to Christ's Authority and Their Causes

The most direct defiance of Christ's lordship is the refusal to include Jews or others in our evangelism because of prejudice, an all too common phenomenon in our midst. Such refusal is reprehensible, not only as disobedience, but also as a violation of the very nature of the gospel and of the spirit of Christ. The rebellion, however, has other causes as well.

In the American scene, we are constantly tempted by social pressures to permit popular opinion to claim our allegiance, thus displacing Christ as Lord. This is a particularly great problem in a democracy. The opinion of the majority is regarded as decisive and determining, and so it easily becomes an idol.

This point can be illustrated very easily even in church life. When the old Federal Council of Churches, for example, was confronted with the question of the possible membership of Unitarians, a decision which would have a direct relationship with the confession of the lordship of Christ and would have a bearing upon obedience to the Great Commission. Fortunately, the United Lutheran Church, which then had a consultative relationship with the Federal Council of Churches, took a firm stand which undoubtedly had a great deal of influence with the final decision not to compromise. Popular American opinion which idolizes "breadth" and also the tendency to make ecumenicity an end in itself were powerful factors opposing this decision.

In the matter of our responsibility under the Great Commission of including the Jews among all others in the universal gospel witness of the Church, the great deterring factor again has been popular opinion. The witness to the Jews has been regarded a violation of the traditional boundaries between Roman Catholics, Protestants, and Jews—boundaries which have become inviolate and sanctified by custom, as Will Herberg has so well pointed out. Any violation of these boundaries is regarded as un-American and as an act of bigotry. Moreover, church leaders and agencies frequently have entered into relationships and cooperative ventures with the Jews which they feel will be embarrassed by any witness. This certainly became evident at the Evanston Assembly.

Nor have our theological trends been immune from influence by various social pressures. Dr. Hendrik Kramer, the well-known Dutch theologian of missions, once raised a question to the effect that he wondered if the relationship of the American churches with the Jews might not be a key to the understanding of the American theological situation. Certainly, it is a barometer of our obedience to Christ, and a very devastating one at that. It is dealing with the Jews that we most directly indicate our readiness to acknowledge the lordship of Christ.

One theological trend which is commonly associated with a refusal to evangelize Jews is a weakening in Christology. For example, Frederick C. Grant, in his recent book *Ancient Judaism and the New Testament*, expresses the wish that "we might give up all 'missions to Jews' and begin to understand one another." Does he mean to classify efforts to include the Jews in the normal witness of the Church under "missions to Jews"? If so, he is deliberately prejudicing the case by using the most offensive term he can for all forms of witness. More important, he has no difficulty in excluding the Jews because earlier in the book he has already relegated Christology to a secondary place. If one gives Christology a definitely secondary position, it becomes just one more secondary development under theism, whereas the Judaistic answer is another which is equally valid. "Christ and Him crucified" is no longer the essential message, and evangelism becomes pointless. This Christological aspect might in part explain Reinhold Niebuhr's rejection of evangelism of Jews. Quite apart from this issue, Niebuhr has been accused on occasion of making Christ little more than a symbol.

To summarize, in the matter of our obedience to Christ under the Great Commission with respect to the Jews, we face direct and maximum pressures on every side. We face pressure within the church itself, tremendous pressure, as demonstrated at Evanston. We face pressure on the part of the Jews, who don't want any witness. We face pressure on the part of many Americans who have no particular religious interest and to whom this is merely an issue of patriotism or of cultural breadth. Hence, if there is any point at which we are likely to be embarrassed by our relationship with Christ and our obedience to Him, this is the one.

B. Some Indirect Challenges to Christ's Authority

It is the actual practice of the churches with respect to the Jews that we most commonly find indirect challenges to Christ's authority in the Great Commission. The matter which we are discussing, however, is just one facet of our total American missions responsibility. When the Jews are neglected, that neglect is frequently part of a larger indifference which is particularly directed toward those among whom quick immediate returns to the outreach of the churches are not likely. The American success philosophy plays an important part here. "Does this pay, and are we wasting our money and effort by doing this sort of evangelism?" is the common question.

Many of our congregations are facing an influx of people of different economic, racial, cultural, and religious backgrounds. Home mission boards frequently encourage such congregations to stay where they are and minister to people as they come. Yet, too often, the extension programs of the churches at large appear to be run on a quite different basis by the very boards which urge the congregations to remain and minister to their respective communities. New congregations are commonly planted only in the most favorable situations. This almost suggests a double standard. Looking at the American missions picture in general, isn't it true that, by and large—and this is a generalization to which there are notable exceptions—we tend to serve the intercultural groups only when they are thrust upon us by circumstances which are not of our making? In establishing new work, we select very carefully; but, when these people are thrust upon us by circumstances, we must become heroic and minister to them because we can't escape them with a clear conscience. Do we really care for people of intercultural groups unless we are willing to initiate work among them in order to minister to them?

At a mid-century home mission conference held at Omaha, Nebraska, Dr. H. Conrad Hoyer and Dr. Theodore E. Matson proposed that a certain percentage of extension funds be set aside for use in blighted areas. The proposal did not have an immediate bearing upon the outreach to the Jews, but it nevertheless had important implications in providing a principle that could eventually affect the attitude of the churches to all neglected groups.

The arguments used to counter the proposal of the two leaders proved to be exceedingly interesting. They did not make their appearance until after the conference. There came, for example, the charge that the boards were expected to dissipate all their extension funds in non-productive areas. This accusation was amusing, in that the two leaders had suggested the setting aside of a very modest percentage for use in blighted areas. Another argument used in rebuttal was that the boards should not weaken their financial potential in unlikely areas, but serve only the best until they have become strong. Then they will be in position to care for the blighted areas. The argument sounds like that of the business man who promises to stop and care for neglected concerns when he has earned his first million. We shall never reach the end of the favorable fields, and we shall never get to the neglected groups by such a policy. Hence, we see that our responsibility to the Jews is not something unique in itself, but that it is part of the American missions picture in our country as well as part of our total responsibility to our Lord under the Great Commission.

It is curious that Reinhold Niebuhr, in opposing evangelism of the Jews as futile because it didn't bring results, was only vocalizing something that the churches too often are declaring in their practice. As an additional argument, Niebuhr pointed to the offense previously given to the name of Christ by persecution, thus adding greatly to the difficulty of the task. Now, we would heartily agree with him on this second point; but in the contention that the task is futile in terms of results, we cannot be so sure. It is quite characteristic of Niebuhr's philosophy that there is a note of pessimism in it. He seems to be far more impressed with the potency of sin than with the power of God. In his analysis of human perversity, he has been a prophet; but, in a matter such as sanctification, he speaks with little conviction.

In answer to the pessimism indicated widely in the churches in their practice and stated openly by Niebuhr, we must remind ourselves that all authority has been given to Christ in heaven and on earth, and it is on that basis we are sent. This authority not only involves Christ's right to give a mandate to His Church but it also proclaims the active power by which Christ renders the work of His followers effective. This is particularly significant in connection with the outreach to the Jews which is associated with such pessimism. Paul boldly declares the gospel to be the power of God unto salvation for both Jew and Greek, and for that reason he is not ashamed of it.

To be sure, we must not by any means minimize our guilt with respect to the Jews, nor the consequent difficulty in reaching them. Nevertheless, recognition of past sin does not justify doing the Jews the further injustice of withholding from them the saving gospel of Christ. Our dilemma rather should cause us to turn to God for help.

It would be well to remind ourselves, in this connection, of the close relationship that modern scholars have observed in the Scriptures between creation and redemption. In both, God is making something entirely new; but, even more significant for us here, He is able to bring light and order out of darkness and chaos. Genuine repentance, which is the work of the Holy Spirit, when seen against a dark background, sometimes becomes a powerful witness.

God's call to service came to Moses and to Paul even though their early efforts had created chaos that seemed beyond repair. Since Moses had rashly slain an Egyptian overseer, nothing further could be done until the reigning Pharaoh had died. Undoubtedly, Moses spent forty years in agony and misery, feeling that he had personally committed his people to further suffering through his rashness. This seems to have been reflected in the sense of inferiority and defeatism which he manifested when God called him to go and deliver his people. We see something of the same thing in the Apostle Paul as he contemplated his past persecution of the saints, and yet the Lord declared him to be a chosen vessel and used him mightily once he was transformed.

There was chaos in the lives of both of these men, but to both the Lord gave assurances of His abiding presence and help. Possibly that is the secret of their lives. They had come to the end of themselves; their lives had become a chaos. Now God could act. In a sense, isn't that the situation in which we find ourselves as a Christian Church in our relationship with the Jews? On the surface, it is a hopeless situation and certainly beyond our power of solution. In the light of what we have done, speaking from a purely human viewpoint, Reinhold Niebuhr is right. And yet, do we have the right to take the position that the situation is beyond repair? Let us not forget the Lord's anger when Moses declined to do God's bidding even after repeated assurances of guidance and help. Just because we have complicated matters by our folly, we are not entitled to claim immunity from the inclusiveness of the Great Commission so as to declare the claim of Christ upon the Jews null and void. This would be arrogance rather than repentance and humility.

A second indirect challenge to Christ's command has come through a denial that Jesus ever spoke the Great Commission. Usually the mandate is associated with Matthew alone, but it actually appears in other forms in Mark, Luke, and Acts. Critical scholars have questioned all four forms as being authentic sayings of Christ: the form in Matthew, because it contains the "Trinitarian formula," which is thought by them to be a later theological development in the Church; the form in Mark, as it is part of a commonly questioned ending of the Gospel; and the forms in Luke and Acts because these books are in a sense secondary sources. Yet a good many of the same scholars hold that the Great Commission accurately represents the intent of Christ as seen in the numerous expressions of His universal saving purpose scattered throughout His teachings. Moreover, it would be extremely difficult to conceive of the tremendous dynamic and unity of purpose of the disciples apart from some specific mandate from their Lord.

Finally, some, by referring to the alleged example of the Apostle Paul, claim that the Jews are not included in the responsibility under the Great Commission. It is pointed out that Paul shook the dust from his feet and turned away from the synagogue. This is a dangerous generalization. Paul did this only in local situations when he was rejected by specific groups. Under such circumstances he would indeed depart and turn to the Gentiles; but, in the very next city, he would again go first to the Jews. This he did all the way to Rome, the last recorded city where he proclaimed the gospel. This was always his procedure.

In this connection it is also helpful to note that, even though an early Christian leader had a specific commission to minister to a certain group, he nevertheless felt an obligation to serve all others as well. Thus, Paul, who was commissioned to be the "apostle to the Gentiles," never forgot the Jews; and the leading apostles who had been with the Lord and who seem to have felt a particular responsibility to the "circumcision" (Gal. 2:9), nevertheless also eventually became witnesses to the Gentiles. Their specific calling was never seen to limit a total responsibility. It is particularly significant that Peter, who had been entrusted with the gospel to the circumcised (Gal. 2:7), was the very one who was sent to the Roman Centurion Cornelius and thereby provided a decisive demonstration of God's concern for the Gentiles.

C. The Witness of the Church to the Lordship of Christ

The Church must bear witness to the Jews in deed and word in obedience to her Lord who in love is seeking to save and bless them. Their rejection does not alter His claim upon them as their Lord. For them to declare, "We will not have this man to reign over us" (Luke 19:14), does not in the least diminish His right to their faith and allegiance. God, and not Israel, has exalted Him, as it is so powerfully stated in the well-known *kenosis* passage: "Therefore God has highly exalted him and bestowed on him the name which is above every name, that at the name of Jesus every knee should bow, in heaven and on earth and under the earth, and every tongue confess that Jesus Christ is Lord, to the glory of God the Father" (Phil. 2:9).

Even more pointed are Peter's words announcing Christ's exaltation by God following the rejection and the crucifixion: "Let all the house of Israel therefore know assuredly that God has made him both Lord and Christ, this Jesus whom you crucified" (Acts 2:36). We recall that many in the Jewish audience were pricked to their hearts and said, "Brethren, what shall we do?" To this Peter responded, "Repent, and be baptized every one of you in the name of Jesus Christ for the forgiveness of your sins; and you shall receive the gift of the Holy Spirit." Very significant are Peter's subsequent words to the Jews: "For the promise is to you and to your children and to all that are afar off, every one whom the Lord our God calls to him" (Acts 2:39). Jesus Christ is the Lord of the Jews whether they will accept it or not, and we who share with them the guilt of the cross must make it clear in deed and word that the meaning of the cross is redemption and forgiveness, and not hate and persecution.

Apart from the confession of Christ, the Church of Christ does not exist, and she is the true church in the measure she does confess Him. It is strange that the confession fails most often at the point at which the grace of Christ is most clearly and directly challenged. This should be a particular concern to Lutherans who staunchly profess to believe in justification by grace through faith. As Lutherans examining this issue concerning the Jews, we must remember we are a confessional church, and we must study the issue in the light of the lordship of Christ.

Those of us who are involved in ecumenical relationships must bear in mind that both the World Council of Churches and the National Council of Churches have a minimal confessional basis—Jesus Christ as divine Lord and Savior or Jesus Christ as God and Savior. Discussions in ecumenical circles on this whole matter of responsibility to the Jews often tend to be at sea because the issue is not always clearly related to the declared basis for ecumenical relationships and cooperation. Lutheran representatives have a responsibility to insist that this be done in this and in all other issues of joint concern. The question must be asked in each instance, "How does this matter stand in relation to Jesus Christ as divine Lord and Savior?"

II. THE GREAT COMMISSION IN RELATION TO OTHER EXPRESSIONS OF GOD'S SAVING PURPOSE

The subject we are discussing, "The Great Commission and the Proclamation of the Gospel to the Jews," was one of those chosen for the Bossey Theological Consultation. I must confess that I was disturbed when it was assigned to me, because it limits discussion among American Lutherans who, over more than a decade, have been developing a somewhat broader base for an outreach that will include the Jews. Dr. H. Conrad Hoyer, understanding very well the problem involved, graciously gave his consent to an extension of the scope of the discussion so as to include the American convictions.

A study of the experience of the Church in the time of the apostles will show that simply the possession of the Great Commission was not enough to clarify the thinking even of the apostles in terms of the range of their responsibility. It was only as the Commission stood in relation to two other vital factors that the full picture of the universality of God's saving purpose and work became clear.

A. *The Three Areas or Expressions Which Clarify the Inclusiveness of the Gospel*

Among the three areas or expressions we shall consider, there is good reason for taking the Great Commission first in our discussion. The Commission is an expression of the eternal saving purpose of God's sovereign love, a love which embraces all and is universal in its scope. In a special sense the Great Commission finds its ultimate sanction in the Father, for Christ clearly indicates that His authority is delegated—"All authority in heaven and on earth has been given to me. Go therefore . . ."

The second expression of God's universal redemptive purpose lies in the deed itself—the saving deed of God in Christ in history. This would include the divine dealings with the chosen people, the revelation, the incarnation, the atonement, and the triumphant resurrection and ascension. It could likewise be said to involve, as acts in history, the gift of the Holy Spirit and of the "good news" of the gospel, which is not mere message but the very power of God unto salvation to all who believe. Until the deed was complete, Israel as a people was directly involved as apart from the nations. Once the deed was complete, however, it was delivered from all particularities and historical contingencies. The deed was now universal in its bearing. Man has been redeemed in Christ by God's action alone and man is consequently justified by grace alone through faith. Hence, any distinctions between men other than faith simply have no meaning in the light of the deed.

Through the deed, which obviously centers in the person of Christ, all barriers between men are removed, including especially the wall of partition between Jew and Gentile. Incarnation and atonement, to begin with, are meaningless apart from the unity of the race. Likewise, men are made one in the "New Adam" and in the "Israel of God." In relation to the deed, there now can be neither Jew nor Greek, neither slave nor free, neither male nor female. The law and the prophets are fulfilled. Israel as such, as a national entity, can never return to the category of the deed because all historical contingencies and all national prerogatives no longer exist there. Those who try to force the Jews as such back into the area of the redemptive deed, where they were previously used for our salvation, really deny that the deed is complete and do away with justification by faith.

For the sake of clarity, let us recapitulate. The primary expression of God's universal saving intent through the gospel is that which we find in the Great Commission, for it sets forth God's eternal purpose of sovereign love which embraces all men. (In using the term *sovereign love*, we are not implying a doctrine of universalism.) Secondly, we have discussed the deed of God in Christ which, to be sure, took place in history in connection with the People of Israel, but which, once completed, was freed from all accidents and contingencies of history and all human prerogatives. Hence it became a second universal in its bearing. Its blessings are now free to all men, and I say that Israel in its national sense or the Jews as such can never place a special claim on this category, except that, in the light of their labors, they were entitled to receive first of the blessings (Acts 13:46). The Gentiles can boast of but one thing, and that is precisely that they have nothing of which to boast and no prerogatives to claim. As such they are ideal candidates for this grace, but only as they acknowledge their poverty. We must understand this and also understand the Jewish problem in connection with it. Peter was well aware of the relative positions of

Jews and Gentiles with and without historical prerogatives respectively. Hence he said to the Jewish
Christians in connection with their relation to the
Gentiles, "But we believe that we shall be saved
through the grace of the Lord Jesus, just as they will"

The very universality implied in every phase of
God's deed in Christ confronts us with the inescap-
able responsibility to witness to the Jews as to all
others. To leave them out as the sole exception is to
give credence to prerogatives which we thereby acknowledge to be equal to or superior before God to
God's own deed in Christ. It is to deny the complete-
ness of the deed and its universal bearing.

The third expression of God's universal saving purpose, in which the Church is commanded to partici-
pate, finds concrete expression daily in the arena of
history. It is the work of the Holy Spirit through the
Word in specific lives. Here all individual as well as
social differences and problems are faced and dealt
with, as are also the accidents and contingencies of
history. None are evaded. Here we see the Spirit
granting personal faith and bestowing justifying and
sanctifying grace. Here there is differentiation in the
Church of God—Jews and Gentiles, bond and free,
male and female, rich and poor, ruler and subject,
black and white—each with his gifts and God-given
vocations. Here also there is differentiation between
groups and denominations, in theology (considering
its multi-dimensional character), in culture and practice, and in the roles they play under God.

Were a sizable number of Jews to respond in faith
to the gospel, Israel as a people could well fall into
this area in terms of vocation along with other nations. Because of their gifts and calling, of which God
does not repent (Rom. 11:29), and because of the
advantage of a unique historical perspective, it is not
inconceivable that God could use them to fill the
whole world with fruit (Isa. 27:6) so that it would
be like life from the dead. We insist, however, that
this would not be a return to Israel's previous role
in the preparation of salvation. It would be a case of
believing Jews being called by the Spirit to vocation
along with all the redeemed from all nations. There is
but one Church.

Having said this, however, it must be stressed that
the grace of gratitude ought never to permit Gentile
Christians to forget that salvation is of the Jews, as
our Lord declared, and that the sufferings they have
endured as a chosen people are not to be regarded
lightly. Such gratitude does not destroy the equality
of the Kingdom. As Dr. Jakob Jocz has so well expressed it, "At the very most, the Jew would be
primus inter pares, 'first among his peers.'"

The need of a third testimony to God's universal
intent was well illustrated in the experience of the
apostles. Even though possessing the Great Commission and having had the most intimate contact with
the deed that would be possible, there was still lack
of understanding as to the inclusiveness of the gospel.
It took the witness of the Spirit through specific cases,

such as that of the Roman centurion Cornelius, of the Ethiopian eunuch, or of a believing Gentile such as Titus, whom Paul brought in person to Jerusalem, to convince the church that the gospel is for all without distinction, by faith apart from works. Note Peter's immediate leap from the specific to the universal as he spoke in the house of Cornelius: "Truly I perceive that God shows no partiality, but in every nation any one who fears God is acceptable to him" (Acts 10:34-35).

These three expressions of the universal character of the saving gospel, involving two universals and one specific, have not been brought together artificially by American Lutherans. The power of John 3:16 lies in this that it unites these three: "For God so loved the world"—that is the eternal purpose of sovereign love; "that he gave his only Son"—that is the deed which is universal as the expression of all-inclusive love; "that whosoever believes in him should not perish but have eternal life"—that is the work of the Spirit in any specific believing individual. In developing its Christian approach to the Jewish people, the National Lutheran Council fortuitously followed this general pattern in challenging the member churches and their congregations. To begin with, the stress was upon responsibility under the Great Commission. Then the implications of the "Good News" and of justification by grace through faith (having to do with the deed) were investigated and disseminated through literature and personal contact. Final-

ly, in 1948, a questionnaire was sent out to pastors
to discover how specific individuals had been reached
through the gospel, the results being published and
made available to all pastors.

B. The Interdependence of the Three Expressions

Taken by themselves apart from the others, the
three expressions become easily amenable to distor-
tion. Thus, the Great Commission apart from an adequate concern for the wonder of God's deed in
Christ and for the deep problems of the individual
over which the Spirit of God agonizes, can be applied in a very perfunctory manner. Some people
carry on evangelism pretty much on this wise: they
put the gospel in a dump truck, figuratively speaking,
back up to a likely-looking candidate, dump the
gospel on top of him, and then drive off with satis-
faction, saying, "Mission accomplished!" It is simply
another responsibility or an arduous task to be discharged.

The second expression, the deed of God, is also
easily distorted when taken alone. The implications
of the deed as they pertain to a universal outreach are
simply tremendous. We have already indicated that
the incarnation and the atonement are rejected if
we deny the unity of the race, and also that justification by grace is set aside if human distinctions other
than faith are permitted to enter in. Concerning the
"good news," we could say that it is not good news

unless it is good news for all. Otherwise it would be
bad news for some.

While spelling out such implications at a theological level, we can get so involved and theoretical that
confrontation with the living Christ, a sense of the
urgency of the task, or a grasp of the problems of
the individual, might well be lost.

There probably is not as much danger in the Lutheran Church today as previously, but very often—
and this is a frightful oversimplification—we tend to
be primarily epistle preachers rather than gospel
preachers. Let me illustrate what I mean.

Just suppose that a man knew nothing about drama
and was desirous of becoming informed. He would
naturally begin by seeing a play on the stage. If it
was the first play he had ever seen, and if the pro-
duction was well done, he would doubtlessly be so
caught up in the plot and in the action that he would
be almost identified with one of the players on the
stage. Having seen a play, he would then seek per-
mission to go backstage. There he would interview
the director, the players, and possibly even the play-
wright. He would see how the players rehearse, get
their cues, and come and go, and also how the scen-
ery and the curtains with their ropes and pulleys
work. Thus he would have two essential views of
drama.

We might liken the gospels to the play on the
stage. In them one sees Christ confronting men; and
somehow, before one knows it, he finds that it is he

himself whom Christ is confronting. In the epistles an apostle takes by the hand those who are already believers and leads them backstage so that they can see more fully how they were redeemed and what is God's purpose in their lives. As already indicated, this is a serious oversimplification, as it does not adequately take into account that there are elements of both aspects in both gospels and epistles and a dual purpose has been served by both. Yet, in justice, it must be acknowledged that there is a predominating emphasis in each case, pretty much as we have described it.

In Luther's day the drama on the stage had become pretty much the whole thing. Through his study of God's Word Luther was impelled to go backstage and see if the players were actually speaking the right lines and if the leading roles were being played by the right players. His suspicions were confirmed and his extended visit backstage amply justified. Unfortunately, we as Lutherans have tended to spend most of our time backstage ever since. We have been greatly occupied with the ropes and the pulleys—in short, with mechanism and with process. We generally preach on the gospels and frequently deliver marvelous epistle sermons on them.

That an overemphasis on mechanics and process has serious dangers, should go without saying. Unconsciously our people might be trying to duplicate a process, however much grace has been stressed.

They can well be asking, "Am I repenting enough; am I believing enough?"

As we well know, sin in its essence has two aspects. First, there is *unbelief,* in which we turn away from God; but, in the same act, we turn also toward ourselves, which is *egocentricity,* the second aspect. Salvation must enable us to get our eyes off ourselves and directed back to God. If our preaching of the Gospel mainly stresses process, it has the same effect as law, causing men to look more at themselves than ever. Somehow, they must be beguiled into looking away from themselves; but they will be so beguiled only when they truly see the living Christ, the crucified and risen Savior. Only the Holy Spirit can enable us so to lift up Christ, for this cannot be explained in terms of mechanics. Nor can it be done, in the final analysis, apart from them, as an opposite school would have us believe. We cannot dispense with sound doctrine and the preaching of the law.

It is intriguing to study the ministry of John the Baptist. He preached the law so faithfully and powerfully that men became thoroughly sick of looking at themselves. But the day came when he lifted hand and voice and pointed to the living Christ: "Behold, the Lamb of God, who takes away the sin of the world!" This was the climax of his ministry.

It is hard to say dogmatically how prevalent the occupation with mechanics and process is in the Lutheran Church today, but I have seen its perils in my own ministry. The reason it has been treated here at length is that such an obsession enormously increases our approach to the Jews, who tend to be more personal and concrete in their thinking than do the average Gentiles. This does not mean that Jews cannot think abstractly. As a matter of fact, they do so superbly. However, there tends to be less personal involvement when they do so than there is with us.

It is a common characteristic of people from the Near East, whether it be Syrian, Armenian, Arab, or Jew, that formal relationships such as business or intellectual discourse are more objective and less personal than among the Gentiles of the West. In personal relationships, however, they tend to be more intimate and warm than we do. I know of a business man who by choice deals exclusively with Jews and of another who prefers to deal with Syrians. Both testified that they have learned how to make friends with these people; and, once friendship has been achieved, they receive better treatment from them than they do from people of their own background.

Simply to have an extended religious discussion with a Jew might be far more meaningless than a person realizes, for it might have been purely formal. It is important, consequently, that we should, through the grace of God, somehow get through to the personal level, where we touch the real man. Once he knows us as a friend, he is far more likely to be willing to meet a Friend of ours. It was a warming experience to hear a Jewish friend say, after talking with him about Christ, "Let me tell you something—I have known you for two years, and I am convinced that you are interested in me as a person and not as just another prospect for Christianity; and any time you want to talk to me about Christ, feel free to do so, even though I can't promise you I'll ever become a Christian." Asked if he was interested in a New Testament, he replied, "If you give me a New Testament, I'll be happy to receive it."

In short, mere occupation with the deed of God in Christ in its mechanical aspects is likely to be abortive in reaching men, and particularly the Jews in our midst. But can anything be more direct and personal than the incarnate, redeeming, and indwelling Christ? What a perversion to make it mechanical and perfunctory!

Finally, the third expression of God's universal concern, the work of the Spirit in the individual life, when considered by itself, can also be perverted. Because this expression takes into account individual differences, it can be greatly misunderstood apart from the two universal expressions. The tendency, paradoxically, is to absolutize certain spiritual experiences or practices, particular charismatic gifts, methods of working, types of church government, specific abstinences, etc.

This brings to mind a street meeting in a Jewish district a number of years ago. A representative of a fundamentalist sect repeated verbatim Stephen's words to the Sanhedrin: "You stiff-necked people, uncircumcised in hearts and ears, you always resist the Holy Spirit. As your fathers did, so do you" (Acts 7:51). Needless to say, there was a riot. Later, in defending himself, the speaker argued he had used nothing but the words of the Scriptures. He was unable to reply, however, when questioned whether he believed the Jews he addressed had been given the same opportunity to know Christ as had the members of the Sanhedrin of Stephen's day who had experienced direct contact with the Lord.

Another man worked out a technique which he systematically used in every Jewish home he visited. He succeeded in closing the Jewish doors in three cities to Christian visitors.

The National Lutheran Council study of 1948 revealed that Jews had been reached through every means of contact normally employed in the work of the Church. It was discovered that the effectiveness of a given approach varied with circumstances which could be described in a general way. To be sure, there are certain taboos to be avoided—certain ways in which a person can offend unnecessarily, but there are no real shortcuts. God does give individuals certain gifts which help in making contacts, such as the "green thumb" that enabled a pastor to make many fruitful contacts through his beautiful flowers. Few could duplicate his experience, however, and one could not therefore universalize such a means of approach.

Rather, the lesson of experience is that the most important thing is to go as the Lord commands. I have observed a number of cases in which a pastor was disgruntled because efforts to include the Jews in the outreach of his parish had proved abortive. The day came, however, when word was received from the pastor that the first Jewish person had been reached for Christ. Usually, that was only the beginning. I am convinced that there was continued fruit, not because the pastor and congregation had learned a sure-fire technique, but rather that, through the initial experience, they had come to believe that the gospel is indeed the power of God unto salvation for Jew as well as for Gentile.

If the third expression of God's universal purpose through the work of the Spirit in individual lives can be distorted by separating it from the preceding universal elements, we can say also that, when seen in proper context, it can prove tremendously decisive in demonstrating God's concern for groups that are being by-passed. By exposing the instances in which people are neglected, it arrives at inclusiveness by a different route than the two universal expressions. This is precisely what the Holy Spirit accomplished in the case of Cornelius. We would be justified in asking if the Spirit has given any indication in our day that our churches should be reaching out to the largely neglected Jewish population in our land. The answer of the Spirit confronts us in the presence of confessing Hebrew Christians in our very midst.

I should like, however, to recount an incident which occurred in one of our own metropolitan churches. Is it permissible to tell a story in a theological presentation, or is it only in the Scriptures that theological meaning can be conveyed through accounts of historical incidents?

A Jewish refugee artist, who had settled in one of our metropolitan centers, was engaged in a struggle for existence in a strange land. He was not too busy, however, to go out each Sunday morning in quest of peace with God. Judaism had not satisfied his soul, but family and community pressures had hindered an investigation of Christian teachings in his mother country. Now he was free to search, and each Sunday morning he went to a different church.

One Sunday morning the artist found himself in a Lutheran Church located on a side street. The message from the Word of God that morning deeply gripped him. Moreover, something in the pastor's personality and attitude also drew him. He said to himself, "There is a man in whom I can confide!" Rather shy, he slipped out following the service without speaking to the pastor. He was so excited over his discovery, however, that he did not realize he had failed to notice the address or even the appearance of the church. In a heavily-populated area with many churches, a sanctuary on a side street entered at random would be hard to locate again. He remembered only two things: As one entered the church, the stairway to the narthex went up transversely, and he remembered the pastor as a small man. Hence, he started a new quest for a church with a stairway inside which went up sideways and a little pastor who preached God's word so powerfully.

The quest lasted from the first Sunday in Advent (around the first of December) until the first Sunday in April. On the first Sunday in April, he opened a church door and, to his joy, the stairway went up sideways. Out came the little pastor and preached another powerful sermon. This pastor later proved to be a real friend and blessing to the artist.

After a year of instruction, the artist was baptized. He rejoiced and said, "This is my real birthday!" It happened one day that the artist and pastor were talking about the circumstances which had led to faith in the life of the former. They discovered an interesting thing. On the Sunday that the artist first found the church, the pastor was not the regular minister of the congregation. There was a vacancy, and he was there preaching a trial sermon. The entire time the Jew was searching for the church, the pastor was not there. In the meantime the pastor received a call from that congregation, accepted it, and arrived on the first Sunday of April to preach his initial sermon as the regular pastor. On that Sunday the Jewish artist found the church again. Had he found it sooner, he possibly would have thought he was in the wrong building. Asked if he thought that this conjunction of events was an accident, the artist replied indignantly, "No! It was the Holy Spirit!" In

the early church, the Spirit found it necessary to demonstrate in the case of Cornelius His concern for the
Gentiles; in our day He has found it necessary to
show, by such a specific case as that of the Jewish
artist, His concern for the Jews.

When the universal elements are stressed largely
to the exclusion of adequate consideration of the specific needs and problems in individuals and groups
with which the Spirit of Christ is concerned, it becomes hard to appreciate why work in one area
should be more difficult and apparently less fruitful
than in others. This lack of understanding is a major
reason for widespread neglect of witnessing to Jewish people. Are we able to say that anyone has had a
fair opportunity to make a decision unless the gospel
has been brought to him in sufficient power and
clarity to at least begin to counteract the negative
witness he has received among so-called Christians
as well as the distorted views and pressures from his
own background? Do we not also owe it to our Lord
to seek through His grace so to present Him to the
Jews through life and Word that the distorted picture they have received of Him may be corrected?

III. MAKING DISCIPLES, BAPTIZING,
TEACHING

A. *That They May Believe and Have Life*

The Jews asked Jesus, "What must we do, to be
doing the work of God?" He replied, "This is the

work of God, that you believe in him whom he has sent" (John 6:28-29). The Jews will not come to faith through mere discussion of our so-called common "Judeo-Christian heritage." Nor is baptism optional in the light of the price it entails. When the man born blind was excommunicated for his confession, Jesus challenged him further to a higher rather than a lesser confession.

It is easy, however, for the witness to be demanding without regard for the responsibilities which such uncompromising witness causes to impinge upon his own life. Jesus said, "It is enough for the disciple to be like his teacher, and the servant like his master" (Matt. 10:25). The one who becomes a witness or teacher of the gospel to the Jews, must ask himself, "Is it enough if they become like me? Would the brand of faith I represent be of the kind which would bear up under the persecution and ostracism which Jewish believers in Christ will inevitably experience from people of their own background as well as from un-Christian Christians? In what degree does my faith rest on my favored position in society, and in what measure does it rest in Christ? Am I fully cognizant of that which the step will cost them, even though I know that the Lord will enrich them a hundredfold for anything they surrender for His sake? Am I willing to be friend, or father, or mother, or brother, or sister to them, especially if those they have loved the most turn against them? Am I willing to work with the people in my own congregation in

order that new believers may have a worship home
where they will truly have an opportunity to know
what it means to belong to the family of our Father
and of our Brother? Am I willing to love and defend
Jews even if they don't respond?"

B. Teaching Them to Observe All Things

What is it that the word of Christ has to teach Jews
for daily living? Surely, He confirms much that is in
the Old Testament—in fact, takes much of it for
granted. What would be unique and helpful for the
Jews is not so much in detailed content as in funda-
mental principle and spirit. In seeking to convey this
principle to interested Jews who are willing to take
the time, I like to retell the story of Joseph, treating
it in a somewhat rabbinic fashion. Joseph was a
savior to his people and so closely identified with
them that his embalmed body was kept at his re-
quest as a token that God would visit them and
bring them back to the land God had promised to
their fathers. Even more, Joseph revealed in surrender to God the only principle or spirit under
which Israel would ever know true freedom under
God.

It might be of interest to you to hear this interpretation. Possibly you will disagree with it violently.
However, would you patiently hear it through to the
end, regarding it as a piece of temporary scaffolding? When we have finished, feel free to throw away

the scaffolding; and then see if any of the insights or conclusions survive through their own intrinsic validity.

It is usually not wise to begin at the end of a story in order to discover the outcome, but in this instance it is fully justified. Joseph himself explains two times (Gen. 45:4-11; 50:19-21) that his God-given calling is to preserve life, to care for his own to the end, and, finally, in death, to be the very symbol of their future under God (50:24-26). A glance at Joseph at the beginning quickly shows he is far from being ready to save his wicked brethren and the arrogant Egyptians, and that he consequently must grow a great deal. His development is indicated by his reaction to God's word, which he encounters in three pairs of dreams, his and others'.

We see Joseph at home, disliked for reporting his brothers' sins and for being the object of his father's favoritism. The first pair of dreams pertained to himself and his own future exaltation. With teen-age occupation with self, he possibly would not have been interested in dreams of others or about others. Certainly, he did not inquire into the purpose of his future exaltation. If the first dream infuriated his brethren, did he have to tell them the second one? Was it necessary that he wear the heir's "coat with sleeves" when he was sent to visit his brethren in the field? Morally superior to his brethren, he thus far showed little of the spirit that would be necessary to save them. We might say that he still was, to a considerable degree, a creature of impulse, of fleshly impulse. We could liken this period to "the esthetic stage," Kierkegaard's first stage on the way of life—an unrestrained expression of the natural impulses. Joseph indeed disciplined the grosser impulses, but not the tendency to irritate his brethren. His immaturity, however, did not justify their selling him into Egypt.

In Egypt, faithfulness through God's grace to the Lord and even to human masters, however unjust, eventually brought Joseph to the point of interpreting favorably the dream of Pharaoh's imprisoned butler with a consequent hope of release. Why did God let the butler forget? Was Joseph not yet ready to save his brethren and the Egyptians?

Note that Joseph revealed a deep sense of responsibility. As a slave, he had a vocation to fulfill. Potiphar had been kind and had promoted him; hence Joseph could not sin against the God who was helping him through his master. Wrongfully imprisoned, he still had a responsibility to the keeper and a vocation even as a prisoner. He had now grown so that he would listen to other people's dreams and dreams that were not about himself. The butler and the baker had been committed to his care and he was responsible for them; hence he interpreted their dreams for them. The dreams were about judicial decisions about to be handed down. When Joseph had favorably interpreted the butler's dream, he asked for a favor in return for a favor. He told of the injustices he had experienced; and, although he announced to the butler the latter's imminent pardon, he wanted justice for himself.

Observe in this summary the recurring emphasis upon responsibility, gratitude, judicial decisions, exchange of favors, and pleas for justice. Joseph's vision of service seems to be limited to those to whom or for whom he has specific delegated responsibility. This corresponds with Kierkegaard's second stage—the ethical stage. There is something grand and exalted about this stage. But what would have happened to Joseph's brethren if Joseph had been released and exalted at this point at which he was thinking largely in terms of strict responsibility and demanding justice for himself? What would have happened to the Egyptians under whose vicious social system he had been enslaved and unjustly imprisoned? A legal mind is no fit instrument for God's life-giving grace. God's major work was safest with Joseph in prison.

God's schooling for Joseph went on two more years. Then Pharaoh had a pair of dreams which none could interpret. The butler remembered; Joseph was called, and the dreams were interpreted. Seven years of plenty followed by seven years of famine—how elementary to a man who had administered superbly, not only the great household of the captain of the Pharaoh's guard, but also the national penitentiary! But now he stood personally before the one man who could release him, and he had done

Pharaoh a favor. Interviews with rulers of empires are short—time only for one thing! Why not ask a favor in return for a favor, and go free?

But Joseph had grown. Now another person could have dreams—dreams about an Egyptian people under whom Joseph had suffered and toward whom he had no humanly-defined responsibility, and Joseph would listen and be concerned, and he would forget himself and try to save them. At that point Joseph was set free and exalted.

Kierkegaard's third stage, the "religious," is too weak. In the Scriptures, it is far greater: love, forgiveness, grace, and living through dying! Love knows no limits. The dream, Joseph later found, pertained to the need of all men, including his own family, for the famine was universal (41:57). Now God could bring down Joseph's brethren; Joseph would forgive and show love, and Joseph would learn that God had changed their hearts, too.

But the story of Joseph is the story of his people. Before his death, Moses warned his people that they should not go on doing what was right in their own eyes, especially after entering the Promised Land (Deut. 12:8 f). Rather, they should do what is right in God's eyes (Deut. 12:25, 13:18). But what does the Book of Judges tell us of subsequent generations? The very same story! "Every man did that which was right in his own eyes!" This was Israel's childhood and adolescence in terms of service to God, with fleshly impulse or free self-expression as the keynote.

Then, with the leadership of Samuel, David, and subsequent prophets and kings, and especially with the lesson of the Babylonian captivity, the ethical stage developed. Israel is still in that stage today. Nevertheless, during that stage the disillusioned Gentiles had dreams, and Israel had an answer to those dreams. From Israel went forth a gospel message that brought pardon to some, but judgment to others. But Israel, except for a minority, wanted none of the message for herself, but rather demanded justice for her portion. She has appealed for remembrance to us Gentiles who saw the promised pardon as come true; but, like the butler, we have forgotten her, not two years, but two thousand years. Israel has remained silent as far as any world-wide witness during the greater part of these two millennia. The butler, she says, stopped her. But isn't the real basic explanation the fact that God wants even the guilty saved and nourished, and that a legal spirit would rather punish where God wants to give life?

It would be untrue to every conviction which I possess to end this presentation as though it were a purely objective theological analysis. I stand here for the hope of Israel, longing for the day when the Jewish people will finally see God's purpose for them in Joseph, in Moses (who also died a living death for others, and was exalted by God), in Jeremiah, and finally and fully in their Messiah who vocalized once for all the secret of the realization of that purpose when He said, "Truly, truly, I say to you, unless a grain of wheat falls into the earth and dies, it remains alone; but if it dies, it bears much fruit" (John 12:24). This was not idle theory: He demonstrated it in His own person.

One longs for the day when finally the Jews will be beguiled by the vision of their Messiah into looking away from themselves. Forgetting to barter favors for favors and to demand justice at all costs, may they see the troubled dreams of an agonized world; and, embracing the need of the guilty host nations, discover that they have at the same time embraced the world's need and have also found therein life for their own stricken brethren. This is their God-given vocation among the nations in terms of service, and also true greatness.

This, then, in the light of the story of Joseph, is the essence of that which the Word of Christ has to teach the Jews. But how will they know it if we do not love them enough to tell them of it? Like Moses, however, we say, "Who am I that I should go?" But the Word of the Lord comes back, "But I will be with you"—or in the closing words of the Great Commission, "And lo, I am with you always to the close of the age."

Now feel free to remove the scaffolding!